Clinical Counselling in Voluntary and Community Settings

Clinical Counselling in Voluntary and Community Settings provides an overview of the development of counselling in a world of managed care, where resources are tight and professionals are stretched to their limits. Experienced contributors from a varied and diverse background cover issues including:

- The place of voluntary and community organisations in society at large
- The nature of counselling in voluntary and community settings
- Containment and holding
- The nature of the client group and its effect on clinical work.

This book provides theoretical and practical advice of interest to both experienced practitioners and students considering a placement with a voluntary counselling organisation.

Quentin Stimpson is a UKCP registered psychotherapist and a UKRC registered independent counsellor. He runs a private practice as a psychotherapist, counsellor and supervisor and lectures on various counselling programmes from Diploma through to BA and MSc/MA levels. He is the course leader for the MA in Psychotherapy and Counselling at Bournemouth University.

Clinical Counselling in Context
Series Editor: John Lees

This series of key texts examines the unique nature of counselling in a wide range of clinical settings. Each book shows how the context in which counselling takes place has profound effects on the nature and outcome of the counselling practice, and encourages clinical debate and dialogue.

Clinical Counselling in Context
An Introduction
Edited by John Lees

Clinical Counselling in Primary Care
Edited by John Lees

Clinical Counselling in Further and Higher Education
Edited by John Lees and Alison Vaspe

Clinical Counselling in Pastoral Settings
Edited by Gordon Lynch

Clinical Counselling in Schools
Edited by Nick Barwick

Clinical Counselling in Medical Settings
Edited by Peter Thomas, Susan Davison and Christopher Rance

Clinical Counselling in Voluntary and Community Settings

Edited by Quentin Stimpson

Brunner-Routledge
Taylor & Francis Group

HOVE AND NEW YORK

First published 2003 by Brunner-Routledge
27 Church Road, Hove, East Sussex BN3 2FA

Simultaneously published in the USA and Canada
by Brunner-Routledge
29 West 35th Street, New York NY 10001

Brunner-Routledge is an imprint of the Taylor and Francis Group

Typeset in Times by Keystroke, Jacaranda Lodge, Wolverhampton
Printed and bound in Great Britain by TJ International Ltd,
Padstow, Cornwall
Paperback cover design by Lisa Dynan

This publication has been produced with paper manufactured to strict
environmental standards and with pulp derived from sustainable forests.

British Library Cataloguing in Publication Data
A catalogue record for this book is available from the British Library

Library of Congress Cataloging-in-Publication Data
Clinical counselling in voluntary and community settings / edited by
Quentin Stimpson.
    p. cm.
Includes bibliographical references and index.
    ISBN 1-58391-155-3 (alk. paper)—ISBN 1-58391-156-1 (pbk. :
alk. paper) I. Counseling—Great Britain. I. Stimpson, Quentin.
    BF637.C6C456 2003
    361'.06—dc21   2003007347

ISBN 1-58391-155-3 (hbk)
ISBN 1-58391-156-1 (pbk)

Contents

Notes on contributors

Sue Cottrell is a psychotherapist, counsellor and supervisor with a full time clinical practice in Brighton. As well as her individual therapy and supervision work she also works with couples and groups. In addition, Sue supervises counsellors at the Brighton Lesbian and Gay Switchboard Counselling Project. Sue has worked as a group supervisor and trainer at PACE (Project for Advice, Counselling and Education for lesbians and gay men), and as a part time lecturer on the MSc in Therapeutic Counselling at the University of Greenwich. She originally trained in Gestalt therapy in the late 1980s and now works from an integrative perspective. Sue has an MSc in Integrative Psychotherapy and is BAC accredited and UKCP registered.

Alison Elgar has worked as a counsellor for nearly 11 years. She has worked in a variety of settings, mostly within the voluntary sector. She came into counselling through the field of infertility therapy, working with couples, both lesbian and heterosexual, who were experiencing fertility problems. From there she remained within the medical field, moving into the area of HIV counselling. She has worked as a counsellor in the mental health field for a number of years, working with adults and young people. Until recently she worked exclusively with lesbians and gay men at PACE (Project for Advice, Counselling and Education for lesbians and gay men). Alison now runs a full time private practice as a counsellor and supervisor. Her core training is in psychodynamic counselling and she is a BAC accredited counsellor.

Paul Gordon is a member of the Philadelphia Association. He worked for many years at Open Door, a psychotherapy service in North London for adolescents and young adults, and at the Arbours Crisis Centre. He now works as a psychotherapist and supervisor in private practice and in one of the Philadelphia Association's community households. His articles and reviews have appeared in *Free Associations*, the *British Journal of Psychotherapy*, *Psychodynamic Counselling* and the *Times Literary Supplement*. His book, *Face to Face: Therapy as Ethics*, was published by Constable in 1999.

Derek Hill, a volunteer marriage guidance (MG) counsellor for some years, left the British Council to become an MG and then a Relate supervisor. Work as a Relate counsellor trainer led to his appointment as Head of Counselling and subsquently Head of Practitioner Training. In the past decade Derek has contributed to the development of Relate's Certificate in Marital and Couple Counselling and to the establishment of a programme of postgraduate studies. A BAC trustee and member of its Complaints Committee, he has also had a hand in the development of the UK Register of Counsellors and of NVQs for counselling. He became a Fellow of BAC in 1999 and retired from Relate at the end of that year.

Linda Machin has been actively engaged in research and practice related to bereavement since 1979. She has a number of publications including *Looking at Loss* (Pavilion, 1998) and *Working with Young People in Loss Situations* (Longman, 1993). Since becoming a lecturer at Keele University in 1990 she has continued to focus on issues of bereavement and is currently undertaking research which explores the nature of the diverse range of response to loss.

Gertrud Mander was a supervisor, tutor and course organiser at the Westminster Pastoral Foundation from 1980 to 2000, and is now in private practice as a psychoanalytic psychotherapist. She has published numerous articles on psychodynamic counselling and psychotherapy, and her book, *A Psychodynamic Approach to Brief Therapy*, was published by Sage in 2000.

Ela O'Farrell is a teaching fellow on the DipSW at the University of Kent at Medway. For many years her practice experience was in statutory social work with children and families and other client groups, both in direct work and management. More recently, she has counselled children and families, working from an integrative/ psychodynamic orientation.

Christopher Robinson is director of Waterloo Community Counselling, an inner city counselling service in South East London. He works in private practice as a psychotherapist and clinical supervisor. His background is in community mental health work and he is presently training as a psychoanalyst at the Institute of Psychoanalysis.

Quentin Stimpson is editor of this book. He is a UKCP registered psychotherapist and a UKRC registered independent counsellor. He runs a private practice as a psychotherapist, counsellor and supervisor, and lectures on various counselling programmes from Diploma through to BA and MSc/MA levels. He is the course leader for the MA in Psychotherapy and Counselling at Bournemouth University.

Eva Stolte is a UKCP registered psychoanalytic psychotherapist working in private practice in Southsea. She is a member of the Association of Group and Individual Psychotherapy (AGIP), where she trained in the late 1980s. Her interest in and involvement with counselling has been through her work as supervisor for Portsmouth Counselling Service and her role as clinical consultant and supervisor for Chichester Counselling Service, where she has also run several assessment work-shops for counsellors. Before and during her training in psychotherapy, Eva worked for 20 years for social services in a variety of settings, mainly in the field of adult psychiatry.

Nicholas Tyndall is actively involved with Cruse and Victim Support. He has worked for the Prison Service, National Marriage Guidance Council (now Relate) and Cruse Bereavement Care. He trained with Marriage Guidance and was involved in the beginnings of the Standing Conference for the Advancement of Counselling, the predecessor of BACP. He became BACP's first Chair and is now a Fellow. He is the author of *Counselling in the Voluntary Sector* (Oxford University Press, 1993).

Acknowledgements

I would just like to thank the many clients and colleagues who have, over the years, challenged and stimulated my thinking and practice as a psychotherapist and counsellor.

I would also like to thank the contributors to this volume for their interest in the project and their continuing support through what at times has been a slow and arduous process.

Introduction

Quentin Stimpson

The contributors to this book come from varied and diverse backgrounds, both in terms of their experiences of working in community and voluntary counselling services and in relation to the clinical theories that they draw upon, although they all share a belief in the importance of non-statutory, community-based counselling service provision. It is hoped that this belief will have helped to enliven the issues and questions that the different authors discuss and that their diversity reflects something of the wide range of community and voluntary counselling services that operate in contemporary Britain. No attempt has been made to reconcile the differing viewpoints presented; rather the tensions between different perspectives are allowed to speak for themselves with the aim of encouraging, and stimulating further thought and debate in those who read the text.

The book follows an implicit structure, moving from historical and contextual issues (relating to the place of community and voluntary sector counselling services) through to research and evaluation and then, finally, coming to focus on a range of clinical issues as they affect non-statutory counselling agencies. The first three chapters (by Christopher Robinson, Nicholas Tyndall and Derek Hill) situate and contextualise community and voluntary counselling services within British society. In particular Chris Robinson (Chapter 1) offers a tantalising glimpse of the political potential of community counselling services, which is all the more interesting in the light of the increasing pressures upon statutory services as they try to cope with the ever-rising demands being placed upon them (from both government and services users themselves).

Chapters 4 and 5 consider the increasingly important question of the place of research within counselling services. Linda Machin (Chapter 4) describes how she used a case study approach to evaluate issues relating to good practice in a bereavement counselling service, while Ela O'Farrell

(Chapter 5) focuses upon her research into the effects of third parties on the therapeutic space in work with children. While both of these chapters are quite specific, nevertheless they raise issues that extend beyond their own contexts, including, of course, the importance of clinically relevant, practitioner-based research. That voluntary and community-based, non-statutory counselling services are also having to find a way of articulating cogent reasons for their continued existence (and funding) in today's world is an acknowledged fact of life. It is exciting to see examples of small-scale, contextualised reseach that seek to make a difference to practice and counselling service provision by utilising methodologies that draw upon more qualitative and reflexive ideas (in an effort to remain relevant to practitioners, while at the same time demonstrating the level of rigour that underpins the thinking and work being undertaken in these contexts). An additional and important point to note is that, while these two chapters are specifically research orientated, this is not to deny that practice is a form of research. Thus, to the extent that all the chapters deal with the writer's reflective (and reflexive) engagement with their experiences working in voluntary and community counselling services, so what they are also doing is undertaking a form of practice-related research, or, what Lees (2001) has termed 'reflexive action research'.

The book then moves on to address a range of clinical issues as they arise within community and voluntary counselling agencies. In Chapter 6 Eva Stolte considers the issues relating to the assessment of clients presenting for counselling (a perennially important topic). In Chapter 7 Gertrud Mander addresses both the positive and negative aspects of holding and containment within organisational structures. Sue Cottrell and Alison Elgar (Chapter 8) aim to raise important questions about whether counselling services should be specific and specialised or generic, via a consideration of the issues around the provision of counselling services by gay/lesbian counsellors for gay/lesbian clients. While not offering any easy answers to what is, after all a difficult question they do explore the strengths and limitations of a wide range of solutions to the dilemma. In addition to the arguments which they present, the reader may also want to consider the possibility that providing counselling services for specific client groups run by counsellors from those same groups may actually be a way of avoiding (or, blurring) something important: i.e. the issue of difference (and the extent to which we are all different from each other).

Paul Gordon (Chapter 9) picks up the implicit theme of the previous chapter, namely how to address difference. It provides a critical reading of the place of theory and technique in counselling practice. Gordon challenges us to consider to what extent theory and technique are a way of avoiding encountering the client in their difference and uniqueness. In the final chapter I look at community and voluntary based counselling services from a postmodern perspective and consider how they could fill an important role within the continued development of counselling in contemporary society.

In conclusion, this book provides a snapshot of some of the themes and issues facing community and voluntary counselling services today, as well as a reflection of the thoughtful and creative thinking and practice to be found in those contexts. The contributors emerge as thoughfully engaged practitioners who are concerned with the constant re-evaluation of their practice in order to enhance the work which they undertake with their clients. It is hoped that this window on to the struggles and challenges of working in voluntary and community counselling services will inspire and provoke further thinking (and evaluation) among those who read this volume as they consider how the issues raised might translate into their own working contexts and practices.

Reference

Lees, J. (2001) Reflexive action research: developing knowledge through practice, *Counselling and Psychotherapy Research* 1, 2: 132–38.

Chapter 1

The place of community and voluntary organisations in society at large

Christopher Robinson

Introduction

In this chapter I consider the role of community and voluntary organisations in society at large. I begin by defining what is a community or voluntary organisation. I then consider the historical perspective of such organisations – their relationship to the communities in which they develop as well as to the statutory sector or state-provided care services. I specifically consider here the growth of community-based counselling services and their value to society and local communities. I then discuss some of the particular qualities of community and voluntary organisations – their contribution to the development of services for local populations and their function in society at large in providing change and innovation. Finally, in balance to the qualities of such organisational activity, I look at some of the drawbacks and weaknesses of community and voluntary organisations, which may hinder their development and success.

I write this chapter from the perspective of someone who has worked in this sector for the majority of my working life and in doing so have come to value the particular atmosphere of innovation and hope that characterises community and voluntary organisation activity. At the same time I have a very practical awareness of the problems encountered by these organisations that weaken their potential contribution to society.

What is a community or voluntary organisation?

There are a number of ways of defining what a voluntary organisation is, or what differentiates it from other organisations. I shall consider a number of possible definitions below. (For the sake of ease and because my interest here is in smaller, community-based voluntary organisations,

I use the term 'voluntary organisation' to refer to a community-based voluntary organisation rather than large national charities or pressure groups, which, although they may have similarities with community-based organisations, have a different, larger scale function in society.)

Community organisations: statutory and non-statutory

There is a variety of community-based organisations that provide social or medical services to the population of that community. These organisations can be separated into statutory or non-statutory services. Statutory organisations form part of a statutory or government-provided system such as the National Health Service or local authority provision: they have certain defined statutory duties to perform for the local population, i.e. the provision of health or social care. The fundamental duties of such organisations are usually defined within a legal framework laid down by government. For example, a local, community-based social services team will be working within certain defined duties laid down within the most recent legislation adopted by government.

Non-statutory organisations, on the other hand, provide services that are not necessarily defined within a specific legal framework. These organisations are described as 'voluntary', 'charitable' or 'independent' sector organisations. A complication to this division into statutory and non-statutory organisations is that some statutory organisations may provide services that they are not necessarily legally obliged to do. For example, a local NHS clinic may provide a family therapy service, the provision of which is not within its statutory duties but is additional and complementary to them. Furthermore, a non-statutory or voluntary organisation does of course provide services within a legal framework (the Charities Act, etc.). However, the important point for the purposes of this chapter is that the service provision in this sector can be more freely defined and changed according to the particular aims of the organisation.

Community organisations: the voluntary organisation

Having distinguished the non-statutory from the statutory organisation, the voluntary organisation can be further defined. A voluntary organisation is therefore an independent organisation that acts outside the sphere of government-provided health and social care provision.

It is voluntary in the sense that its activities can be defined by its own members, rather than by government and legislation. The voluntary organisation is constituted as a charitable organisation and will have a guiding constitution or Memorandum and Articles of Association that is monitored by the Charities Commission. Additionally, the voluntary organisation may be legally set up as a limited company and its activities will therefore also be monitored by Companies House, which oversees all limited companies (the majority of which have commercial functions as their primary activity).

It would seem that the voluntary organisation has a two-fold function of being 'charitable' – not being motivated by commercial profit but by what might be termed social profit or benefit – as well as having some of the qualities of a commercial venture in its need to provide services responsive to the demands of the community it identifies. In doing so it must possess what might be seen as the commercial qualities of responsiveness and innovation, i.e. responding to 'gaps in the market' (the market referred to here being the provision of social/health services rather than commercial activity).

Development and growth of voluntary organisations: a general historical perspective

Historically, the role of voluntary activity has been a very significant one in encouraging and enabling the growth of social and health services within communities. It is only in relatively recent years that governments have accepted responsibility for the provision of extensive social and health services. This has been a gradual process over the last 150 to 200 with the initial impetus for the improvement of better social and health services coming from very different sections of society: from the voluntary and charitable activity of wealthy, socially conscious benefactors as well as from the organisation of local and national trades union and social reform organisations committed to improving the lot of their fellow workers. It has largely been the case that, because of the action of committed individuals and groups, the development of what we consider now to be basic individual rights in a modern society such as health care, social care and housing are available to us. Of course, such rights to basic services come about gradually over time due to an amalgam of individual action, social change and political pressure. However, government legislation that solidifies and makes explicit such rights is inevitably influenced by the work already put into practice through local initiatives and individual action. For example, the growth of social housing provision in the 19th century made possible by such benefactor activity as the Peabody and Guinness estates was later taken on by government in the subsequent acceptance of the role of the state in providing basic housing for the economically poorer section of society.

Development and growth of community-based counselling services and the role of voluntary organisations

Voluntary action at a community level has then often been the impetus for larger aspects of social change and development. Within the present development of counselling and psychotherapeutic services, it is interesting to observe how the growth of counselling provision within local communities has occurred in what today we call the primary care sector of GP clinics and community-based services. The provision of 'talking treatments' has tended to be something largely confined to the private sector where economic considerations – the ability to afford counselling or psychotherapy – has meant that less well-off sections of society have had restricted access to this type of psychological treatment (Holmes and Lindley 1989). Psychotherapy services within NHS settings have tended to develop and stabilise over the past 50 years and therefore have been perhaps more generally available. In recent years however they have faced their own difficulties, competing with newer drug treatments and differing views about the origins of psychological disturbance and mental illness.

Shifts within our society's general perception of the value of counselling and talking treatments appear to have encouraged the growth of counselling services in the community. Whilst debate continues over the complex origins of psychological disturbance, in parallel to the sophistication of our understanding within professional circles, there has been this growing general awareness of the value of a psychological understanding and treatment of presenting problems such as depression and anxiety. This seems to be rooted in cultural and social changes, which place greater value on the understanding of our emotional, psychological and sexual lives.

In this context, at 'grass-roots' level in our society we are experiencing what amounts to a greater demand for counselling services. In essence, there is increasing social pressure to provide alternatives and new approaches. Whilst the demand for effective medication to treat depression, stress and anxiety continues to grow, there is also a demand for non-medical interventions such as counselling. Voluntary organisations have played a role in these changes by publicising the value of alternative treatments and by providing direct services in local communities, particularly in very recent years. For example, the organisation in which I work grew originally out of a local community health project set up to monitor and improve the health needs of the local population. The explicit aim of this group was to improve physical health through health education in areas such as smoking, sexual health and diet. The group found that the people visiting them increasingly wanted to talk about the emotional aspects of their daily lives and relationships and this led to the setting up of a counselling service. In this way, organisations such as my own have managed to develop services that have responded to the changing pattern of demand at community level. Additionally, we are now seeing how these counselling activities are being taken up by the statutory sector through the growth of primary care counselling provision within GP practices.

Whilst this growth of counselling provision at local level would appear to be a solid and hopeful development, a note of caution is necessary. A less promising development is one in which voluntary organisations are in fact filling gaps in social and health provision caused by a restricted NHS and local authority activity due to reduction in government spending. Whilst counselling services are growing, we are directly seeing counsellors in voluntary organisation and primary care settings having to cope with complex psychological presenting problems that are more realistically the domain of hard-pressed psychiatric departments or psychotherapy services. Community-based counselling services are struggling to fill the gaps and often find themselves providing a 'first aid' service when, in fact, more resources than the counsellor can provide are necessary. One hopes that voluntary organisations engaged in this sort of experience will perform an effective function to society by certainly attempting to fill gaps where possible, but also by recognising their limitations they can perform a wider 'consciousness-raising' task: to encourage government action to further improve community-based mental health services.

Qualities of voluntary/community organisations that enable their role in society

Voluntary organisations have a range of qualities that enable them to perform an important role to society in the enrichment of social and health services. I shall discuss what I see as important qualities under the headings below.

Proximity or closeness to community need

Community-based voluntary organisations tend to grow out of the local community – one could say that the community creates them. For example, in the case of my own organisation (as described earlier), the service evolved out of a response to the demand for counselling. Various aspects of the organisational structure of voluntary organisations consolidate the importance of proximity to the community and its needs. For example, a voluntary organisation may have a constitution or governing objective to involve local people in its management, thus ensuring it represents local people. It may additionally be located in an accessible physical setting such as a community clinic or centre.

This suggests that a community-based voluntary organisation has the capacity to 'know' the community and its needs. Of course a local community can be a rather nebulous and diverse entity, especially in an inner city area where many differing needs and different ethnic communities are represented. A voluntary organisation may represent a particular section of that community and be less able or willing to represent other sections. Yet its very proximity to the local people suggests a potential capacity to reflect the diverse population. The recent history of voluntary organisations is one of a general attempt to see such organisations representing local ethnic groups and addressing this in service planning and delivery.

Accessibility and use by the local community

The fact that community-based voluntary organisations are located within communities makes it more likely that people in the community will use their services. This may sound like a truism. However here I am emphasising voluntary organisations as potentially more 'stigma free' than statutory services. Within the field of counselling and mental health especially, yet also more generally, they may feel less threatening to visit. They may be more accessible in a very physical way by being close by – located on a housing estate or community centre – but, more importantly, they can offer a different sort of 'closeness' by being less identified with the often intimidating setting of a hospital or other statutory service. For example, statutory services may feel less confidential. There may be a fear of information being passed around to other unknown government departments or simply the very size of hospitals and the formal, uniformed atmosphere may lead people to fear bringing their concerns about their physical or mental health. In the mental health field particularly there is a common fear of being 'labelled' – being thought 'mad' – if one attends a psychiatric service. These are the common concerns of people who attend community-based organisations – there they may feel more 'at home' and in safer hands. Of course, these fears may be unfounded as hospitals and their staff have similar human concerns as the staff in voluntary organisations. Nevertheless, this is a real factor that is often addressed by voluntary organisations. It is interesting to note here how the recent developments in primary care as the focus of health service delivery seem to mirror a desire to be local, accessible and less institutional.

Proximity and accessibility: a psychoanalytical note

Using the analogy of society as a family, one could describe the role of voluntary organisations as mirroring a maternal function in that family. I would see this as occurring as follows. First, the voluntary organisation has this quality of proximity and accessibility to the community that one could equate with the mother and baby relationship, in contrast to the more paternal and distant relationship of the statutory/state sector. Second, the voluntary organisation potentially meets and processes the needs of the community, providing a 'transitional space' (Winnicott 1975a) between the as yet unstructured needs of the community and the structured framework of the statutory/state sector.

Within this second quality lies the potentially creative role of the voluntary organisation in developing services that fill the gaps and address needs which cannot be met by statutory services. Of course, in describing this role I do not wish to suggest that the statutory sector does not contain a maternal or creative capacity. I am assuming a certain more fixed (and perhaps paternal?) role of the statutory sector in having certain defined tasks.

Problems of Voluntary Organisations in fulfilling their role in society

Voluntary organisations face a variety of problems in fulfilling their role. I would define these problems as falling broadly into the two categories of external and internal problems.

External problems

Securing the resources – funding

Because voluntary organisations in the community are constituted as independent organisations with their own aims and objectives and run by their own members, they exist outside the structured statutory services that are provided and funded by government. Simply put, voluntary organisations have to raise their own funds to pursue their aims. This faces the voluntary organisation with its first obvious challenge – to secure the financial means to carry out its aims. Of course, this problem in itself can be a motivating factor. The belief that resources should be provided by society to meet certain unmet needs is the drive behind the organisation's existence. This necessity to secure funding can therefore provide a voluntary organisation with its particular blend of energy and zeal. Yet it brings with it an insecurity about the reliability and continuity of the organisation's resources. It is true that as voluntary organisations become established over time their funding should also become more consolidated. However it is often the case that as the needs which the voluntary organisation is addressing are not fully established and proven in the eyes of potential funding sources, the reliability and security of resources cannot be guaranteed.

Making the case – relations with external organisations

A related aspect of the necessity to secure resources to carry out the work is the need to work with external agencies such as local statutory services and charitable donors to make the case for the importance of the work undertaken by the voluntary agency. The relationships between the voluntary organisation and the local statutory services can be a mixed affair. To a degree the very existence of the voluntary agency may be a critique of local statutory services; i.e. that these services are not providing something in the community which the voluntary organisation perceives as necessary. However, a more constructive relationship with local statutory service providers can develop with those services encouraging voluntary organisation activity on the basis of recognition of the organisation's particular qualities such as the proximity and accessibility factors discussed above. On this basis the voluntary organisation can act as a channel to influence local funding and service development.

Internal problems

All organisations face internal challenges in the way they organise and carry out their particular functions. The internal challenges facing a community-based voluntary organisation are related to their particular nature of being often small, independent and self-financing and having been set up in a spirit of enthusiasm and zeal. I shall discuss some of the problems that can arise below.

Management and institutional structures – the maturational process

Returning to the analogy of the mother and baby for my purposes here, I think one can understand a particular problem – namely the difficulty voluntary organisations seem to face in developing internal structures and organisational systems – using this idea. Given that a voluntary organisation is set up to respond to a perceived need in a community that has perhaps not yet been fully identified and proven, the organisation has to learn to articulate a clearer definition of that need and develop a service that can effectively meet it. Rather like a mother with a needy infant, the voluntary organisation has to exist in this area of feelings and needs that are not yet fully comprehended and expressed by the services working in that community. The voluntary organisation will therefore exist in a certain atmosphere of zeal and commitment (not unlike the state of maternal preoccupation described by Winnicott (1975b), which gives the organisation energy, yet may work against other forms of thinking which are slower and more structured.

This problem usually manifests itself in the difficulty in setting up internal structures (what we refer to in organisational terms as 'management structures'). An organisation needs to mature and develop to carry out the differing and more complex tasks it faces and this can be a difficult process to achieve. Hopefully, over time as the organisation responds effectively to the external problems it faces, it will develop the structures necessary to carry out the work: rather like the development of infants as they learn how to express their needs and also learn the limits of what they can do.

One psychoanalytical idea that could be applied here is Melanie Klein's concept of the two poles of mental functioning: the paranoid/schizoid and depressive positions (1975a, 1975b). The development of the voluntary organisation may start with its 'birth' in a state of heightened feelings and unstructured functioning as a need in the community is 'felt' or 'seen' but has yet to be fully understood and a service developed to meet that need. This could be thought of as a paranoid/schizoid functioning where feelings are high and depressive feelings (associated with the painful nature of the problem or need the organisation is hoping to meet) are defended against in an atmosphere of zeal (what could be thought of as a manic defence). Gradually the organisation will develop a clearer understanding of the problem or need and will begin to define its limits and set up internal structures that can 'bear' the painful impact of the need the service is meeting. This development could be thought of as a move to a more 'depressive position' functioning with the organisation developing a certain maturity and ability to think in a more complex way about how to meet the needs of its client group.

Funding and developmental challenges – coping with uncertainty

As described in the previous section, the internal challenge that the voluntary organisation faces is to structure a response to the need it perceives in its client group. This necessitates a development in its own structure. Part of this process is the development of internal structure in the form of management structures and other staff support structures. However, because the environment in which the voluntary organisation operates is uncertain – the problem of funding and long-term security – the development of internal structures takes place in the face of particular fears and anxieties, which can again have a certain paranoid-schizoid quality. Namely, the organisation functions with the often realistic fears for its survival or potential capacity for growth. It is important that the organisation finds ways of containing these particular fears within its internal structures to protect the cohesiveness to its services and staff group. Working within an atmosphere of uncertainty may promote a certain excitement to find solutions, yet it also brings with it these more primitive anxieties of disintegration and fragmentation, which can be undermining and harmful for the potential growth of the organisation.

Conclusion

In this chapter I have wanted to think about the role of community-based voluntary organisations in society. I began with a description of such an organisation, differentiating it from other statutory services. I considered the historical growth of voluntary organisations to demonstrate their role in responding to social and health needs in society and in acting as an agent for change and improvement in social and health conditions in society. I considered some of the qualities of voluntary organisations – their proximity and accessibility to local communities – and used a psychoanalytic model to understand their potential role in society. In considering some of the external problems faced by voluntary organisations – securing funding and commitment from other services – this led me to consider the internal problems particular to an organisation needing to develop an internal structure within an uncertain environment. Again, a psychoanalytical view was taken here to illustrate the theme of growth and development and the vagaries of this process.

In conclusion, I believe that community-based voluntary organisations have an important role in society. In essence, at their best they can act as a catalyst for change and development, enabling a community to respond to the changing needs of a population. Within a broad picture of society as a whole, I would see voluntary organisations acting at the edge of society: a place that I have suggested bears a resemblance to the early stages of infant development where the voluntary organisation has a primary parental function. This is a place with a dual nature of potential growth and disintegration. I think it is a sign of the general health and security of society as a whole when this area of activity is supported and encouraged.

References

Holmes, J. and Lindley, R. (1989) *The Values of Psychotherapy*, Oxford: Oxford University Press.

Klein, M. (1975a) 'A contribution to the psychogenesis of manic-depressive states', in M. Klein *The Writings of Melanie Klein, vol. 1: Love, Guilt and Reparation*, London: Hogarth Press.

—— (1975b) 'Mourning and its relation to manic-depressive states', in M. Klein *The Writings of Melanie Klein, vol. 1: Love, Guilt and Reparation*, London: Hogarth Press.

Winnicott, D. W. (1975a) 'Transitional objects and transitional phenomena', in D. W. Winnicott *Through Paediatrics to Psycho-Analysis*, London: Hogarth Press.

—— (1975b) 'Primary maternal preoccupation', in D. W. Winnicott *Through Paediatrics to Psycho-Analysis*, London: Hogarth Press.

Chapter 2

The nature of counselling in voluntary and community settings

Nicholas Tyndall

The tradition of voluntary work in Britain stems from Victorian phil-anthropy and developed throughout the 20th century. It is deeply embedded in the social services. Indeed it has been estimated that almost a third of the population gives some time every month to one or other voluntary body (Smith 1997). This tradition has included the setting up of voluntary organisations to meet specific perceived needs. Samaritans, for instance, began out of concern about rising rates of suicide. Cruse started as small self-help groups of widows, the name drawn from the Old Testament story of Elijah and the widow of Zarephath (1 Kings 17).

Victim Support arose out of a sense that the criminal justice system lacked understanding of the plight of victims and neglected their needs. Large numbers of other voluntary agencies have been formed to address the needs of groups with particular physical or medical conditions. A characteristic of such bodies is that they have a strong sense of mission, with their motivation often generated by people who have personal experience of the needs being addressed, either in their own lives or through close friends or family members. Many of these bodies start as self-help groups formed by sufferers. Others are set up by doctors, ministers of religion or other professionals who are confronted with gaps in service provision for those they are trying to help.

Whatever the starting point, there is an acute awareness of the importance of having a place or person available for people with specific concerns to turn to, and this ensures a focus for clients and workers alike. Clients select an agency for its perceived experience and competence in their type of need. They are likely to perceive a voluntary organisation as having expertise in its own subject, a recognised public presence and a care and concern which is free of commercial considerations or statutory control. As for the workers, they volunteer because at some emotional level they identify with the phenomenon which the agency represents. For instance, many people volunteering to be marriage or Relate counsellors are aware of family issues which have given them an intense interest in the dynamics of family relationships. A lot of those who apply to become grief counsellors have a deep awareness of bereavement issues arising from vivid memories of their own painful loss of relatives or friends. Many Samaritans have known depression or suicidal feelings. For many volunteers then there is a perfectly valid element of personal exploration and making sense of their own life journey. Indeed it is common for such workers to assert that in addition to helping their clients they too have grown in understanding through their work with the agency and its clients.

The specific focus of these agencies provides a clear sentience, or sense of belonging and identification, for those involved. With most of the work being done by people who are unpaid, other motivating factors come into play such as altruism, a need to be part of a purposeful group or loyalty to a cause. This can give voluntary bodies a different feel from profit-making organisations. By way of example, voluntary bodies are notoriously bad at going out of business once their aims have been achieved, or at amalgamating with other agencies with similar objectives. This is not to infer that all voluntary bodies are inflexible. Sometimes there is pressure from other client groups or funding bodies to change the focus, which may be done, The Marriage Guidance Council changed its name to Relate to acknowledge that many of its clients came with problems that were not specifically marital. Cruse expanded its remit from widows only to include all bereaved people, though it has since resisted client pressure to offer counselling over forms of loss which do not involve death, such as divorce or physical incapacity. Victim Support has recently widened its remit to include people injured in road accidents where no crime has been committed. Samaritans now place greater emphasis in their publicity on dealing with despair rather than suicide.

Such adjustments to the focus of agencies' work do not undermine their sentience, sense of mission and keenness to stay in being. Voluntary counselling organisations continue to flourish. They can take pride in being caring agencies in an age when caring is often seen in pejorative terms. They can concentrate in their work on putting people before theory or techniques, offering integrative therapy as advocated by O'Brien and Houston (2000). Clients exhibit confidence in many of the agencies. Volunteers continue to apply as helpers, motivated by identification with the mission of the agency as well as by the lure of self-development.

Emergence of counselling

The term 'counselling' was first adopted in Britain in the voluntary sector, specifically in the National Marriage Guidance Council (NMGC). Describing the beginnings of the voluntary marital agencies, John Wallis, one of the pioneers of counselling in England, chose the title 'someone to turn to' (Wallis 1968). This phrase encapsulates the aim of many of the voluntary organisations that mushroomed in the second half of the 20th century. The term Counselling was first used by Carl Rogers (1942) at the University of Chicago. His client-centred philosophy emphasised the need for a listening and non-judgemental approach to clients that aimed at exploring their problems in an atmosphere of 'unconditional positive regard' and helping them to find their own means of resolution.

Counselling has become a widespread response to people experiencing all sorts of stress and difficulties in personal relationships who seek someone to whom to turn in their dilemmas. A range of services is offered to clients in the voluntary sector such as specialist information and advice, practical or financial assistance, and opportunities to meet in social or self-help groups. These traditional forms of assistance have been available since the early days of Victorian charity in organisations such as the Family Welfare Association (FWA). Today such help meets the needs of many clients either partially or wholly. However, in the mid-20th century, bodies like FWA and NMGC became aware that good advice and practical help often proved unhelpful or even counter-productive to clients. Likewise referrals of clients with, for instance, domestic problems to specialist professionals could prove ineffective. Clients seemed increasingly to find relief merely in having time to talk to an empathetic person about their difficulties. Hence these agencies began to recruit and train people who would concentrate on giving such time and attention, and the term counsellor was gradually introduced (Lewis *et al.* 1992).

Counsellors were trained to see themselves as the primary agent of treatment, enabling clients to unravel their troubled thoughts, gain support in their trials and tribulations and reflect on courses of action. In some instances referral to a legal, medical or financial specialist might seem desirable. If so, the counsellor and client will discuss how, when and where to refer and the counselling may continue concurrently. By the 1970s counselling itself had become the main modus operandi of many of the voluntary agencies.

Furthermore in many of these agencies counselling began to take precedence over other aspects of service provision. This was partly because of the pressure brought by the evident and urgent expressed needs of clients; partly because counselling individuals is much easier to arrange and manage than activities such as setting up training courses or assembling groups of compatible clients. This was apparent, for instance, in the NMGC where the education and training offered, seen as valuable preventive work, developed at a far slower rate than counselling. Likewise the church bodies which comprised the Association of Pastoral Care and Counselling found that the 'counselling' element was more capable of definition and promotion than the 'care' element, so counselling flourished while training for carers lapsed.

In Cruse, the emphasis moved away from social groups, which had mixed aims and open membership with no time limits, to individual counselling where the focus of help was evident. In all these instances, the objectives were clearer, the activity was easier to set up and the workers felt themselves to be more emotionally rewarded.

The practice of client-centred therapy (now more generally referred to as person-centred therapy) as developed by Carl Rogers proved to be highly appropriate as a means of response by volunteers who had been selected as having the core characteristics, identified by Truax and Carkhuff (1967), of genuineness, non-possessive warmth and accurate empathy. Genuineness means an honesty about oneself, a willingness to be open about one's own character and life difficulties and a continuing ability to develop insight into the behaviour of oneself and others. Non-possessive warmth demands care and concern, but with a degree of detachment which prevents one taking over other people's problems: the tricky balancing act of having one foot in the clients' turbulent seas and the other foot planted on the firm ground. Accurate empathy implies an understanding of clients' problems which is deeply held but yet free from any bias or assumptions.

Not all people with good intentions have such qualities and any counselling agency must pay heed to ensuring an effective selection system. There are various reasons for not selecting applicants. Some would-be volunteers have no clear understanding of what the work entails. Some prove to be poor listeners; some have a missionary zeal to share a belief system or impart the lessons from their own experience or life style. Some, though suitable in all other respects, cannot guarantee the commitment of time. Some are students of counselling; indeed with the mushrooming of counselling courses in further education establishments, an increasing number of students are seeking training attachments in voluntary agencies, many primarily to gain counselling practice.

Selectors have to be wary about accepting students whose experiences or maturity render them inappropriate for the agency. They must ensure that there is congruence between the requirements of the training course, the agency and the student on such issues as supervision, confidentiality and caseloads. They must also be discerning about potential recruits who have themselves experienced the phenomenon which the agency addresses – bereavement, divorce, despair or some psychiatric or physical condition – and have not yet sufficiently distanced themselves from that experience. These applicants may well quite genuinely feel that they have worked through the trauma and come to terms with its fallout. However for some, if accepted, the training or subsequent involvement with clients arouse unexpected, hidden or unresolved feelings that are a painful reawakening for the counsellors themselves and which distort the way they hear their clients. It is wise to delay accepting such candidates. By contrast, those who have been through the mill themselves but have sufficiently distanced themselves to be able to listen to their clients' experiences without identifying them with their own, bring an added dimension of maturity to their counselling.

Once selected, the volunteers receive training in counselling skills. Most agencies using volunteers have developed their own skills training programmes, though some rely on external courses provided by other training bodies or educational institutes, but all the agencies are likely to provide training relating to their own specialist focus. This specialist training not only informs the trainees about the nature of the issues with which they will be dealing, but also acts as an orientation into the management systems and ethos of the agency. This can be especially pertinent for external students on placement.

An essential aspect of the selection and introductory training process is to make clear the agency's expectations of its volunteers and ensure that each recruit has sufficient time and motivation to meet those expectations. Each agency has its own norms as to the number of cases or counselling hours required of counsellors. Most of them have a programme of follow-up training sessions to be attended, and all are likely to have stringent requirements for counsellors to receive professional supervision either individually or in small groups.

In these days of increasing professionalisation of counselling, it is essential for voluntary organisations with a specific focus to ensure that their volunteer counsellors receive adequate skilled supervision and are monitored in working within that specialised framework. Counsellors with such safeguards are skilled, well-focused good neighbours, 'amateurs' in the original sense of the word, meaning loving, yet working to professional standards.

Types of voluntary counselling organisations

This chapter primarily considers those voluntary and community counselling organisations which rely wholly or mainly on voluntary counsellors to provide their service. Some of the large voluntary organisations, such as those in the child-care field like Barnardo's, are voluntary in the sense of being non-statutory. They mainly employ professionally trained social workers who are paid. Though these agencies share some of the characteristics of those which use volunteers, their standards and practice are more clearly in line with external professional bodies.

There is a difference between those organisations that provide a service giving national coverage with a head office which exercises some control over its local branches, and those that are independent local bodies which are largely autonomous. The former set standards of training and counselling but generally leave the administration of the local service to local committees. Inevitably, indeed appropriately, there is variation in the service provided by branches in different parts of the country, but the aim is that there will be a recognisable uniformity of standard. Some of these national bodies arrange some or all of the selection, training and supervision of counsellors; others rely on the local branches to undertake these activities. Most provide some certificate of accreditation for counsellors from the national body and increasingly these are recognised by an external academic institution.

The standard setting role of national bodies came under increasing external pressure during the 1990s. These pressures mainly came from funding bodies that are looking for some sort of benchmark by which to judge the agency. They also come from referring agencies that require an assurance of competence and seek it in comparison with, for instance, a professional counselling body such as the British Association for Counselling and Psychotherapy (BACP). This creates a tension within the national bodies where not all branches can realistically be expected to achieve the same standards (the availability of finance and professional support varies greatly up and down the country), and where choices have to be made between providing a lower standard of service than desirable or closing the branch down. As the costs of training and supervision escalate, branches that in other respects are good may be forced out of business by national standards which prove too expensive to implement. Regrettably this particularly occurs in deprived areas where services of all kinds are already sparse.

By contrast, other voluntary agencies exist as single independent entities, brought into being by a community group to meet a specific local need, with their own autonomous local management. Some have been set up through the initiative of a church group, either denominationally or ecumenically, some with active support from a local authority. Examples of the former are the Harrow Churches Bereavement Support Service and the Willows Counselling Service in Swindon; examples of the latter are the Open Door in Feltham and the Hounslow Bereavement Service, both of which are largely funded by the London Borough of Hounslow. These small independent local groups are free to set their own requirements for training and counselling, but nevertheless they feel the pressure to provide an external measure of their competence and opt to come under the aegis of a nationally recognised umbrella organisation such as the Association of Christian Counsellors or the Westminster Pastoral Foundation. In these increasingly professional days, local bodies without some external attachment can feel extremely vulnerable.

Strengths of voluntary organisations

Voluntary bodies have a strong sense of corporate identity. In the larger ones there is often tension between the national headquarters and the local branch, but locally there is almost always a sense of belonging and common purpose. Members join because they are concerned, often passionately, about the objectives of the agency, are convinced of its mission and have a belief that they can individually make some contribution to carrying out that mission. Some are motivated by commitment to their community, some by a religiously inspired care for the less well off. As well as a wish to do something for others there is often an expressed intention to explore counselling as a possible extension of personal skill or indeed as a likely future career. More unconscious needs may also be at work, with past hurts or vulnerabilities becoming apparent during the selection process. Many potential volunteers have personal experience of the need that the agency works to meet or combat. Their members may well be bound by a shared ethos that identifies them as 'our sort of people'. This sense of identity draws similar people as potential recruits. Surprisingly, in an age when part-time paid employment is so prevalent, the supply of suitable volunteers continues to be available.

An important aspect of voluntary bodies is their freedom from statutory control. As they are not directly answerable to a public body, they can set their own rules, take more risks and be more pioneering. It is noticeable that many of these agencies are working with socially unpopular issues such as drug dependency, HIV/AIDS and the rehabilitation of offenders. The agencies are acutely conscious of the importance of preserving confidentiality so that they can gain the trust of clients who may have reasons to distrust public authorities. Statutory workers are always conscious of scrutiny by elected members and officers of local or central government and may well feel politically constrained. Voluntary bodies bear their own responsibility, which of course includes being prepared to give an account of their stewardship of public grants. On some sensitive issues it suits public bodies to fund voluntary agencies to undertake tasks which may not be a high priority or which they are not equipped to do themselves. For many years the marital agencies have received substantial funding from central government. The government is committed to 'buttressing marriage', but does not want to be involved directly in work that might be seen as interfering in the private lives of ordinary citizens. It makes regular grants to marriage counselling agencies, monitoring merely to ensure that the money is spent as requested. Similar provisions are made for family conciliation schemes and ex-offender hostels.

An additional aspect of the independence of voluntary organisations is that they have freedom over their selection of clients. This is not easy to manage. In recent years of cutbacks in statutory provision there is an increasing tendency for professionals with heavy caseloads such as community psychiatric nurses to refer unsuitable patients to voluntary organisations. In bereavement agencies, for instance, a voluntary counsellor trained to assist clients with a 'normal' grief may be faced with a referred client who turns out to have a long psychiatric history and whose experience of death in the family occurred some years ago. However, there is no statutory requirement to take inappropriate referrals. Such agencies have to learn to refuse to take clients that they are not equipped to help, and time is well spent on liaison between social services and bereavement agencies (Currer 2001). Potential clients who are searching around for relevant help may knock on the doors of several counselling agencies before finding a response which they feel to be empathetic. People in distress naturally have uncertainty. Seeking help may be a new experience driven by despair. They may ask themselves how they can be sure that going for help may not increase their problems or sense of failure? The initial contact or impression may seem off-putting. Not surprisingly therefore, some clients will not return after an initial session. Others will not keep appointments. One national agency reckons that 18 per cent of unkept first appointments is to be expected (Tyndall 1993).

It is not clear what makes clients opt for or stay with any agency. The first contact, which often occurs by telephone, is crucial. Many clients are unsure what to expect. It is vital that callers feel heard, welcomed and are given enough time and space to believe their needs have been understood. Alas, some agencies rely on volunteers who have received minimal training to take phone calls, so uncertainty by the client may be met by uncertainty from the telephone helper. Those agencies that give priority to putting trained and experienced people on the phone find their care pays dividends in terms of the client's subsequent confidence in the agency.

Premises also have a considerable influence. As far as small counselling agencies are concerned, my own preference is for counselling offices sited in small terraced houses close to town centres, where access is easy and a homely yet purposeful atmosphere prevails. These buildings combine the best conditions of a formal setting with a comfortable, confidential feel. As such they reflect the sort of ambiance which voluntary agencies seek to provide.

Above all, though, the empathy between client and counsellor must be the most significant factor in achieving client confidence and in the possibility of giving acceptable help. Again, the first contact in the counselling room is of crucial importance. This first session is by way of a blind date, with each assessing the other. Though some professional agencies are able to give time and attention to allocating clients to the most suitable counsellor, the practice in voluntary bodies is likely to be more haphazard. Allocation may well be decided by such factors as availability on specific days or times, current gaps in caseloads or even, in agencies where counselling is done by home visits, geographical location.

Hopefully, at first interviews counsellors can create an atmosphere in which client–counsellor 'match' can be discussed and any reservations about mutual compatibility can be met by the possibility of changing counsellors. My experience is that such switching rarely happens. If such a possibility does get openly explored in the first session in a non-threatening fashion, it probably points to a good rapport having already been established. The counter side of the enthusiasm and clear focus of the voluntary bodies is that they are often constrained by lack of resources of all kinds. There is a danger of poor management and financial crises. In present times many agencies find it easier to attract potential counsellors than treasurers, administrators or committee members. Some rely on organisers who receive honoraria or low pay and may be expected to work longer hours than contracted for. Modern communication technology may well be too costly to install or outside the competence of office staff to operate.

A disproportionate amount of time and energy has to be devoted to fund raising. Increasingly, trusts and public bodies respond to any request for money by requiring detailed applications backed by extensive data and statistics. Few funding bodies are willing to contribute to general funds, so grant applications have to be couched as new projects and ingenuity and financial expertise are needed to devise them. Central government departments that used to give annual core grants to established charities specifically to enable them to concentrate on their service provision now also limit themselves to project funding.

In consequence income is often very uneven. For instance, a considerable grant may be received from some source such as the National Lottery that will inflate income for a time-limited period. This time is unlikely to be extended and there may well be difficulty in acquiring funding from elsewhere to continue the project. So worthwhile projects with promising beginnings have to be shut down. Undue emphasis on projects may mean that the core activity has to struggle to survive. Such unevenness of income requires competent financial management, which again is not easy to acquire in the voluntary sector. Self-funding may be a desirable aim but it is hard to achieve. Voluntary agencies have to grapple with the issue of payment by clients. Counselling, being a labour intensive activity, is costly to provide. Even when counsellors are working without payment, there are still administrative expenses, cost of premises, training and supervision costs, travelling and other expenses to be paid to staff and volunteers. A counselling hour may cost anything from £10 to £30. Practices vary in relation to charging fees from clients. Some agencies, such as Cruse, have a policy that clients will not be charged but will invite them in some way to make a contibution to costs. Others set up an initial interview where the suitability of the client and service are discussed and clients are invited to agree payment according to their means. A guiding principle in voluntary agencies is that clients are not turned away through inability to pay, but this can be an uncomfortable issue for many in the sector where the driving force is to meet client needs with no commercial considerations.

The single-mindedness that is an asset in many regards can also have a tendency to restrict the vision of agencies. There may be ignorance of, or a reluctance to embrace, new techniques or professional approaches. Agencies tend to recruit their voluntary workers from a narrow social band (which varies in different areas of the country) and may fail to see the need to extend their service to different groups of clientele, with a resulting under-representation of minority groups in both counsellors and clients. A low priority may be given to networking with other relevant agencies, so inter-agency cooperation and referrals between agencies may not be developed. Supervision and guidance from external professionals, which is often sought at the start of organisations, may lapse as the organisations themselves become more experienced and feel the confidence to go it alone. Finally there is the pressure, financially and organisationally, of keeping up with perceived external requirements in the counselling world such as, for instance, training and supervision. Traditionally most voluntary organisations have relied on trainers and supervisors giving their services free. This has become less possible as the extent and frequency of these activities has increased. Such skilled personnel are not readily available in many places and, where they are, the time commitment has often become so great that their services have to be remunerated. These costs can be heavy. In big national organisations these more rigorous standards are enforced and monitored but in smaller agencies standards are inevitably very varied.

Future trends

The Seebohm Report on local authority and allied personal social services (1968) foresaw voluntary agencies playing a pioneer role which would eventually be taken over by the statutory authorities when the need for the service had been clearly established. The scenario now looks very different. Voluntary agencies, certainly in the counselling sector, have a clear future as government policy is not to afford to provide counselling in the statutory services for many of the categories of client served by voluntary agencies.

The threat to the future of the voluntary agencies comes now from private practitioners whose numbers have increased enormously in recent years. With the growth in counselling courses, and a more established system of regulation through the umbrella associations, it is likely that counselling will be further developed in private practice as well as through the health services. The obvious attraction for clients who can afford to pay for their counselling is that they can go to a counsellor of their choosing, who might have been recommended to them, rather than apply to an agency and be counselled by whoever is allocated. Some private counsellors manage to practise with low overheads and there-fore their fee in some instances is not dissimilar to that asked by a voluntary agency. Voluntary organisations must therefore remain jealous of their reputations. They have the advantage that many of their clients apply as the result of a personal recommendation by an acquaintance or someone in the professions. Other clients come having heard about the agency through the media and organisations with a national coverage take pains to use the media to let their presence be known. Clients will frequently introduce themselves by saying that they had seen two or three notices about the agency or articles in the press which had eventually persuaded them to approach this particular agency. Above all, a voluntary agency can make an impression as a specialist service that has extensive experience of the type of need which motivates the clients.

Just as the counsellors are drawn to work in a service with whose ethos they feel comfortable, so clients apply because they feel their particular condition will be understood. The specialist label gives an assurance that may be lacking when approaching an individual working alone in private practice. By the same token, counsellors in a specialist agency must accept that they will be endowed by their clients with a greater degree of authority than they may feel. Necessary though it is to guard their reputations in the counselling world, the specialist national agencies, I believe, should not be pushed indiscriminately to conform to criteria established by, for instance, the British Association of Counselling and Psychotherapy. Those criteria are important in the private sector where there may be no external monitoring or supervision, but the voluntary agencies regulate their own practice and should do so to standards which are relevant to their specific specialism based on their experience established with many clients over years. There is a temptation to set standards out of reach of most voluntary workers, but if agencies succumb to that they will be in danger of losing the point of voluntary counsellors who have shown in many settings that they possess Carl Rogers's core characteristics of empathy, respect and congruence and can provide a counselling service of high quality.

References

Currer, C. (2001) *Responding to Grief, Dying, Bereavement and Social Care*, Basingstoke: Palgrave.

Lewis, S., Clark, D. and Morgan, D. (1992) *Whom God Hath Joined Together: The Work of Marriage Guidance*, London: Tavistock/Routledge.

O'Brien, M. and Houston, G. (2000) *Integrative Therapy*, London: Sage.

Rogers, C. (1942) *Counselling and Psychotherapy*, Cambridge, MA: Houghton.

Seebohm, F. (1968) *Report of the Committee on Local Authority and Personal Social Services*, Cmnd 7303, London: HMSO.

Smith, J.D. (1997) *Survey on Volunteers*, London: National Centre for Volunteers.

Truax, C. and Carkhuff, R. (1967) *Towards Effective Counseling and Psychotherapy*, Chicago: Aldine.

Tyndall, N. (1993) *Counselling in the Voluntary Sector*, Buckingham: Open University Press.

Wallis, J.H. (1968) *Marriage Guidance: A New Introduction*, London: Routledge and Kegan Paul.

Chapter 3

Clinical work, supervision and management

Derek Hill

> There is also the fact that therapy as a goal is not a part of science. It is an act of human concern. Its effectiveness, however, rests on the adequacy of our validated knowledge.
>
> (Sutherland 1980: 18)

This chapter is written from the perspective of someone with about 25 years of direct involvement in a national voluntary organisation delivering counselling. Had it been written at the beginning of that period a very different analysis of the subject matter would have been offered. Voluntary bodies have changed remarkably during those years, and so too has the author's practice. Hopefully the latter change is in some part due to a growth in awareness, knowledge and skills, but it also results from societal and organisational change. As Clare Winnicott is reported as saying: 'There is no such thing as casework, only casework in a given setting' (Woodhouse and Pengelly 1991: ix).

In Britain, much of today's counselling in community and voluntary settings has its roots in the 'marriage guidance' offered to the public by charities set up about 60 years ago (Lewis *et al.* 1992). The story of the evolution of those organisations, and of counselling itself, is told elsewhere (Cooper and Lewis 1995; Davis and Hill 1995; Dryden *et al.* 1995). What began in some cases as little more than 'acts of human concern' has become the focus of a burgeoning profession supported and facilitated by the activities of specialists in governance, management, research, marketing, public relations and, not least, fund raising. But the fact that some counselling is delivered by extensively trained and experienced practitioners working within highly developed, complex organisations should not be allowed to mask the fact that counselling currently exists at many different stages of development and is provided by organisations ranging from local action groups to national bodies with multi-million pound budgets.

The origins of diversity

In part, the reason for this diversity lies in Sutherland's (1980) notion of 'human concern'. Just as in the 1940s people identified needs in the community that were not being addressed and set about finding ways to serve them, so today the same processes are at work. Some of those initiatives take the form of extensions of existing counselling services or a retargeting of experienced practitioners' work. In those cases there can be the expectation that ethical and effective services will be provided through the application of best practice. Other community ventures may be set up without connections into the world of counselling; their patterns of caring, helping and listening evolving in efforts to match services to needs and, in the process, re-enacting many of the processes by which counselling itself has developed. Some such ventures are quick to import counselling expertise, while others find themselves pressured to formalise and find the means to regulate the psychotherapeutic components of their services when they turn to sources of public funding for support.

Britain's long history of community action, and its idiosyncratic nature, has resulted in a wide variety of counselling services targeted on single-issue client groups; for example, Women Against Rape (WAR) and other services such as those provided by the Westminster Pastoral Foundation affiliates, which are intended to serve people with a broad range of person problems. There is evidence within the sector of philo-sophical differences and of choices being made about the nature of the organisations supporting counselling services. Some ventures elect to operate as small, peer-managed groups of practitioners while others have dedicated efforts to the development of large and complex organisations capable of regional or national service delivery.

A survey conducted in 1998 by the British Association for Counselling demonstrated the diversity which has been described (Hill 1999). It also confirmed anecdotal evidence that there is no generally applicable rule of thumb by which one can relate the degree to which a counselling service specialises in work with a particular client group, the exper-tise embodied in a service, and the size and complexity of a service's supporting organisation. The evidence available suggests that there is no one uniquely good way to ensure that a counselling service sustains professional standards and has a capacity to address the sometimes subtle issues that arise out of a chosen form of counselling practice.

Common issues and specific solutions

Having illustrated what appears to be a rich and creative diversity in the counselling sector, and keeping in mind the fact that the broader purpose of this book is the improvement of the quality and reliability of the services which that sector delivers, two questions arise. First, are there attributes of and processes at work within the sector's casework practices, organisational structures and among its practitioners that transcend its diversity and suggest generally applicable strategies fostering good practice and effectiveness? Second, are there features of that part of the sector with which the author is most familiar which might prompt those working elsewhere to re-examine and modify their own contexts for professional activity so as to make them more conducive to good practice?

It will be helpful to turn again to Sutherland's notion of human concern in order to respond to the first of those questions: that concern has at least two dimensions. First, there is an altruism that can be found in many an organisation's mission statement – an intention to care for others based on a recognition of some particular form of dis-ease in the community, and the deprivation that persists if it goes unattended. Second, and much less commonly made explicit, there is a desire for 'a *mutual* interaction which both the therapist and the patient (or the group or family he was "treating") learned from and changed each other' (Skynner 1989: xxxvi). Skynner goes on to suggest:

> The mental health professional is unconsciously seeking a substitute experience to compensate for something that was missing in his family of origin (for which) he needs social contact . . . with people who do not share the denial or 'blind spot' typical of his own family. But to the extent that colleagues have chosen the work for a similar covert reason, everyone in the profession will share a tendency to deny similar aspects of their relationships. The institutions they jointly form, at first for mutual support and sharing experience, and later to train their successors, will be based by default on a collusion to continue hiding the denied deprivation and resultant need, rather than to explore, expose and transcend it.
>
> (Skynner 1989: xxxviii)

Skynner's proposition is supported by at least one piece of grounded theory research within Relate (Sully 1992, personal communication), by the personal insights of numbers of highly experienced practitioners within the sector who are known to the author, and by the author's own professional experience. Using the findings of a detailed study of American social workers (Lawton 1983), Skynner (1989) goes on to discuss the modes in which service-providing organisations may operate. At the extremes he identifies what he calls the 'vicious cycle of deprivation' and the 'virtuous cycle of mutual nurture'. He describes the cycle of deprivation as the product not so much of the underlying dis-ease (shared with the client group) but of its denial in order to avoid the intolerable pain of loss or neglect that would otherwise be felt. In the same way that cycles of deprivation are sustained, transgenerationally, in families, he suggests that projective identification results in practitioners (parents) perceiving deprivation within the clients (children) rather than within themselves. He contrasts that situation with the cycle of mutual nurture which is established when denial of deprivation is challenged; when inadequacy and inability (through no fault of their own) is acknowledged and the associated pain is experienced; when real needs are understood and efforts are made to satisfy them; and when workers' capacities to give to each other, and to clients, grow.

During the 1990s these ideas have prompted the author to reflect on his own experiences of work in the voluntary sector and to speculate about the processes underlying individual and organisational behaviour. No systematic investigation has been done and the products of that thinking are offered here tentatively in the hope that others will explore and test their experience in their own settings, with equal benefit.

Experience affirms Skynner's way of describing the 'wounded healer' characteristics of practitioners and their interactions. But in a complex organisation in which practitioners work alongside trustees and managers who may have no therapeutic training, is it safe to presume that the non-practitioners' personal deprivations and unconscious motivations are similar to those of the practitioners? Contacts over many years with hundreds of trustees and managers suggest that those who also have experience as practitioners identify with the practitioner culture and bring with them their own expectations, based on past experience, that it is about being 'haves' (cycle of mutual nurture) or 'have-nots' (cycle of deprivation). Some non-practitioner trustees and managers attune to the practitioner culture spontaneously and exert influences that suggest they might be practitioners-manqué. Others, skilful and dynamic, appear less caught up by the specific intrapsychic needs of clients and practitioners and shape their roles so as to become primarily agents for organisational change and growth. They thereby challenge the 'navel gazers' to strike a new balance between the needs of the inner world and the realities, power relationships and politics of society. Of course, there are those who themselves combine those different agendas.

In a large organisation there are benefits in governance and management that result from the different influences of people expressing a variety of personal agendas. Small organisations are perhaps more vulnerable to the potential for dysfunctional conflict that can arise when key roles are used to polarise differences between subcultures rather than to foster inclusiveness and make use of creative tensions. Inclusiveness will be raised as an issue later in this chapter.

Finding counsellors and supervisors

All counselling organisations are faced with the task of recruiting (trainee) practitioners. It is often said that, despite lip service to anti-discriminatory practice, the self-perpetuation of the characteristics of the organisation's practitioner workforce is the most evident outcome. Relate was accused of sustaining a 'pearls and twinset' workforce, and to some degree that may have been true. Perhaps what is more significant in recent years is that the taxi-drivers carrying trainees to Relate's college claimed to know their destination before ever a word was spoken, and in spite of the fact that the trainees are demonstrably an improving reflection of Britain's socio-economic and cultural diversity. Were the taxi-drivers acknowledging what Skynner would expect?

The notion that the members of counsellor workforces share psychological characteristics presents management with an issue. Should Relate and other counselling organisations discriminate in favour of those who have a personal acquaintance with the kinds of deprivation which resonate with that of the organisation's target client group? Predictably, among those who submit applications to Relate, a substantial proportion show evidence of resonant personal problems. However, the selection procedures used by the organisation were shaped to seek out individuals who, first and foremost, have a capacity or potential to function as counsellors. The organisation's trainers have found that the individuals selected can be mapped onto a continuum which ranges from 'strong unconscious motivation related to resonant issues' through to 'empathic response to resonant issues but with other, stronger unconscious motivations'. It has also been found that those linked with the latter end of the continuum bring a positivity to counsellor groups which challenges the 'collusion to deny' and which helps particularly with the organisation's ongoing struggle to free itself from vicious cycles. If there is a conclusion to be drawn, it is that the processes of *self*-selection at the application stage will ensure that any agency with a well-defined service profile will have a significant proportion of candidates evidencing resonant issues. It seems likely that there may be real disadvantages in seeking to discriminate in favour of those candidates rather than giving priority to those who show themselves to have a broader and more balanced range of the attributes needed in a counsellor. But at the end of the day this kind of recruitment policy results in a counsellor workforce with the predispositions that Skynner would predict and which will include individuals who, like Skynner and this author, 'sneaked in by the staff door to get some help without acknowledging my need for it [at the time]' (1989: 169).

Relate has recruited practitioners for training as supervisors (formerly called tutors) since the mid-1960s. By 1980 there was a clear recognition that potential to train as a 'tutor' was dependent upon more than extensive and successful experience as a counsellor, or skills as an adult educator, though both attributes were valued. In the past 20 years much has been written about the supervisory process, and the styles and attributes of supervisors, for example, Hawkins and Shohet (1989) and Holloway and Carroll (1999). Most of that literature has referred to the supervision of the generic counsellor, and much of it has been strongly influenced by the British Association for Counselling and Psychotherapy (BACP, formerly BAC) which was preoccupied by the needs of the independent practitioner. What appears to have been under-emphasised is the role of the supervisor in countering organisationally based practitioners' engagement in cycles of deprivation and in fostering cycles of mutual nurture. Thinking through the requirements of that function makes very apparent the responsibilities of the supervisor for a close liaison with an organisation's governance and management and vice versa, in order to ensure that the resources are available to fuel the virtuous cycle. It also makes evident the need for the supervisors to have experienced and benefited from a mutually nurturing professional environment. These ideas translate readily into the terminology used when discussing the functions and attributes of generic supervisors. However, few of the latter treatments capture the power of the 'collusion to deny' which can be seen so clearly within specialised counselling agencies and which it is argued can exist in the professional contexts of all counsellors. For organisations like Relate, these ideas sharpen thinking about supervisor recruitment criteria, about the need for supervisor training itself to embody the processes of the virtuous cycle, and about the need to define the role of the supervisor in a way that directly connects supervisory activity with that of management and governance in order to facilitate the virtuous cycle.

The 'haves' and the 'have nots'

Discussions about the distinctive and enduring characteristics of large counselling organisations' different centres are a familiar feature of meetings where supervisors get together, or in which managers with regional or national responsibilities meet. Viewed from Skynner's perspective, these discussions highlight two features of those complex organisations. First, the tone and purpose can be used as an indicator of the 'have' or 'have not' culture of the whole organisation, and about the organisational context in which those key workers are functioning. Second, the descriptions offered about individual centres offer insights into the predominant modes of operation of their staff groups which may or may not be syntonic with that of the larger organisation. Mythologies would have it that 'good', 'bad', 'needy' and 'angry' centres and practitioner groups are unchangeable features of organisational life. The idea that those characteristics can serve to indicate the nature of collective responses to unconscious material is both sobering and hopeful; hopeful because the expertise of those groups is to do with shaping therapeutic responses to deprivations. But, as with clients, at times the task may need the assistance of people a step or two further down the road towards a healthy acknowledgement of needs, a readiness to experience the associated distress, and a determination to find appropriate, growth promoting responses.

Piggies in the middle

More insights are available into supervision and the role of the supervisor in Hughes and Pengelly's excellent book (1997). They speak of the supervisor as 'piggy in the middle' and, drawing particularly on experiences within social work and the probation service, quote Middleman and Rhodes (1980): 'The supervisor–worker relationship is *the key* encounter where the influence of organisational authority and professional identity collide, collude or connect.' Referring to the supervisory process, from Brown (1984) they state: 'This managerial–professional duality is often denied or at least obscured by participants but it will always influence the transactions between them.'

As has been mentioned above, historically BACP has adopted a position arising out of its concerns for the practice of independent counsellors and supervisors. Those concerns resulted in the following clauses being included in the Codes of Ethics and Practice for Counsellors:

Counsellors monitor their counselling work through regular supervision by professionally competent supervisors and are able to account to clients and colleagues for what they do and why.

(BACP 1984: A3.3)

The counselling supervisor should be independent of the line manager role. However where the counselling supervisor is also the line manager, the counsellor should also have access to independent consultative support.

(BACP 1990: B3.3)

Successive versions of the Code (1993, 1996a) incorporated the 1990 wording, but this was replaced in the 1998 Code:

The counselling supervisor role should wherever possible be independent from the line manager role. However, where the counselling supervisor is also the line manager, the counsellor must have additional regular access to independent counselling supervision.

(BACP 1998: B6.3.2)

Supervisors contracted to provide supervision for an organisation's counsellors and also to act as a part of the organisation's line of accountability for the casework being done were assisted in complying with the Association's Codes by the wording of its last Code of Ethics and Practice for Supervisors of Counsellors:

Counselling supervision may contain some elements of training, personal development or line-management, but counselling supervision is not primarily intended for these purposes and appropriate management of these issues should be observed.

(BACP 1996b: 3.2)

Nonetheless, while independent counsellors and supervisors are unlikely to have had difficulties in complying fully with those Codes, their colleagues who were organisationally based struggled with:

- distinctions made within organisations between line management, with its 'hire and fire' functions, and other ancillary management functions which are commonly required of supervisors;
- the subordination of management functions to counselling supervision which is defined as the task of 'work[ing] together to ensure and develop the efficacy of the supervisee's counselling

practice' (BACP 1996b: 2.3) rather than the integration of those functions advocated elsewhere (Hughes and Pengelly 1997);

- the requirement that where supervision involves elements of line-management counsellors '*must* have additional regular access to *independent* counselling supervision' (BACP 1998: B6.3.2), since that independent influence destroys the integrity of the line of accountability which prudent governance requires.

In 2001 BACP published a radically different statement about ethics. A revised version of that Ethical Framework for Good Practice in Counselling and Psychotherapy was published in 2002 and adopted by the Association as the replacement for all previous Codes of Ethics. That document recognised the co-existence of different approaches to ethics by considering Values, Principles and Personal Moral Qualities. It also adopted a definition of 'practitioner', which set managers of therapeutic services alongside counsellors, psychotherapists, trainers, educators, supervisors, researchers and providers of counselling skills. Service managers are thus seen to be bound by the same commitment to ethical practice that applies to those directly delivering services – a requirement many, including this author, had pressed for over a number of years. The Framework makes repeated reference to the need for practitioners to make use of 'consultative supervision' and, in a section dealing with practice guidelines, states:

> There is a general obligation on all counsellors, supervisors and trainers to receive supervision/consultative support independently of any managerial relationships.
>
> (BACP 2002: 7)

Whilst probity of practice is discussed (BACP 2002: 9), no specific guidance is offered about which elements of a managerial relationship are inimical if concurrent with a supervisory function.

Hughes and Pengelly (1997) offer a detailed discussion of the balancing act required by the organisational counselling supervisor and the distortions which may occur in the triangles of supervisory functions (focusing on practitioner's work, facilitating practitioner's professional development, managing service delivery) and of participants (service user, practitioner, supervisor). Skynner's (1989) perspective provides a further powerful argument for the 'piggy in the middle' role and for the closest collaboration between practitioners, supervisors and managers in order to establish and sustain virtuous cycles of mutual nurture.

Processes in individuals

Searle's paper 'The Informational Value of the Supervisor's Emotional Experience' (1986) and Mattinson's book *The Reflection Process in Casework Supervision* (1975) describe what is elsewhere referred to as 'parallel process'. Although not universally recognised, the reflection or parallel process is now widely regarded as an important means by which a supervisor can become aware of otherwise concealed aspects of the content and process of a client's communication with a counsellor. What is of interest for the purposes of this chapter is the fact that the processes which those authors describe are based on the proposition that a client's unresolved conflicts, and the associated affect, can find their way into the counsellor and can have a powerful influence on the counsellor's relationships with others. There can be few who have been members of case supervision groups, who have talked with managers, appointment secretaries and receptionists after their contact with clients, or who have found their own families' dynamics disturbed when they are engaged in powerful casework, who can doubt that uninvited influences are at work.

It is important to note what happens within a staff group if these client-specific processes go undetected and unattended. In groups involved in providing counselling for a specific client category, the unresolved conflicts and developmental issues that the clients are troubled by tend to be similar. Those in contact with the clients are thus repeatedly involved in both the conscious and unconscious processes related to working on that focal group of issues. Unchecked parallel processes communicate clients' characteristic repressed material and the associated, unmanageable affect throughout the staff group. That group, itself predisposed to the repression and denial of material related to the focal issues, collusively defends against the introduced material and experiences a collective sense of the intractability of casework and of their own inadequacy and inability. The staff group may begin to perceive itself as embattled and become very close-knit, showing a reluctance to share its work with outsiders. The anxiety associated with its 'cycle of deprivation' may lead to displacement activities that attribute the causes of the group's difficulties to any number of external influences such as budget problems or the policies of the central organisation. Those involved in the counselling of a broader spectrum of client problems are vulnerable to similar processes and to the low morale that results.

If those processes can be recognised and addressed for what they are through the awarenesses of peers and supervisors, a dramatically different outcome can be anticipated. First, the practitioners concerned will be offered the opportunity to address the issues and the distress which the clients (and practitioners) had previously feared to acknowledge (creating a need for the counsellors to give attention to their own personal growth). Second, the particular cases will benefit from the insights into the client's underlying conflicts and needs, and the counsellor's increased capacity to address them. Third, the supervisor, counsellor and peer group will be aware that denial has been challenged and growth achieved. Together those outcomes act against the disposition to sustain a vicious cycle through collusive denial. Over time, the effect can be to convert a dispirited, anxiously active group of practitioners for whom 'burn-out' is a real threat into a contained and creative group of caseworkers. The author claims no startling triumphs in this regard, but does have experience of the positive impact of skilful supervision on the culture of practitioners' groups in which he has worked. There have also been episodes in his own work as a supervisor when individuals and groups have 'turned the corner' as a result of consistent attention being given to the reflection process.

Clients' experiences

Counsellor groups and counselling organisations have been described as being vulnerable to their own particular kind of sickness. They may also face the kinds of organisational problems that are commonplace in other enterprises. It is therefore important to consider the extent to which those issues have an impact on the services delivered and the experiences of clients.

It has already been indicated that excellent counselling, and highly beneficial client experiences, have been achieved in an almost bewildering variety of contexts and organisational settings. Amongst other things, that fact reflects the adaptability of both counsellors and clients, but that adaptability comes at a cost. The distracting effects of physical discomfort, noise, concerns about privacy, and of conflicting responsibilities, will be familiar to many counsellors. These are matters which those responsible for the management of counselling services constantly monitor, and make the focus of corrective action. What is of more concern here are the psychological processes that counsellors may become engaged in, wittingly or unwittingly, which limit their capacities to adapt to their clients' needs. Some of those processes are specific to the individual counsellor and may be rooted in unresolved personal issues, skill and knowledge deficits, or inadequate professional support. Further personal development work, training, and appropriate supervision are commonly used to deal with those constraints on a counsellor's availability to clients. The processes which can limit or distort a counsellor's capacity to work effectively, and which are less tractable, are those which bind the individuals to their peer group, organisational culture and profession. They may involve belief systems, collusive denial, patterns of organisational defence, unresolved ethical dilemmas, or social contexts antagonistic to therapeutic work.

The dynamics of the processes involving collusive denial have been described earlier and the means to free a counsellor group from them have been indicated. The means to release counsellors from their constraining group responses to the other kinds of issues mentioned are similarly demanding on the individuals concerned and call for the skilful and insightful leadership. That leadership may come from within the group, but the experiences of the other caring professions suggest that change is often initiated when deficiencies in services to clients are detected externally and, also, that leadership to effect change is most often brought in from outside.

So what would the clients' experiences be when a counselling service is distorted by a group response to some such issue? Individual clients may find their counsellors caring, skilful and empathic, but collectively their experience would show that casework had 'blind spots': for example, racist practice, homophobia, denial of abuse, blaming management for service deficiencies, compromised confidentiality, disengagement from social action addressing community problems. A moment's reflection on the history of social services in England will show how difficult it is to identify the causes underlying collective behaviours, and the complexities of work to replace those behaviours by responses which serve clients' interests better. That work is made all the more difficult because the practitioners involved may be convinced that existing practice offers a 'best fit' with their clients' needs.

This discussion might lead some to see counselling services as more part of the problem than of a solution. Perhaps the redeeming feature is that the counselling profession, and the other caring professions, have frequently found themselves at the leading edge of action to uncover beliefs, prejudices and practices, prevalent in society at large, that result in services which fall short of a full and realistic response to those who, for one reason or another, are living disrupted or disadvantaged lives.

Voluntary organisations

These pages have called heavily on the author's personal experience and no claim is made to do more than reflect on the changing nature of one corner of the world of counselling in community and voluntary settings. It may have been noted that in spite of the author's involvement in the voluntary sector, relatively little has been written about the particular issues faced by its organisations and the volunteer counsellors who work within them. As was indicated at the start of the chapter, a different emphasis would have been given to the topics 25 years ago. Then, charities and their volunteer counsellors were to a large extent free agents. This endowed them with a vitality and freedom to experiment that some think is lacking today. That freedom also gave rein to some highly idiosyncratic forms of 'management' and provided the individual volunteers with scope to pursue their own interests and serve their own needs. There were those who said that volunteer counsellors were unmanageable in the 1980s.

So what has changed? First, counselling has become a professional activity. While there were many very skilful counsellors in the 1970s, the *general* level of training and of individual skills, knowledge and awareness have increased significantly.

Second, professionalism has brought with it a closer attention to accountability, standards, ethical practice and to partnership in inter-disciplinary approaches to community problems.

Third, consumerism has resulted in members of the community refusing to take services on trust. Today it is commonplace for a counsellor to be asked about their training and qualifications, for clients to want to know what they are going to be offered before they enter counselling, and for the expectation to exist that a complaint will result in more than a sympathetic acknowledgement.

Fourth, legislation has been introduced that applies to the activities of charities and which give them responsibilities very similar to those of commercial and public sector organisations. Equal opportunities issues are now a major preoccupation of voluntary organisations.

Fifth, the Charity Commissioners now exert a much more powerful influence over charitable bodies and the way they conduct their activities. Today, trustees' responsibilities and liabilities are considerable. The role is no longer the sinecure it was once thought to be. Greater accountability has affected the work of all involved in charitable bodies.

Sixth, access to public funds is no longer a matter of submitting a persuasive application to government or a local authority. Grants have largely disappeared. Access to public funds is now much more likely to be associated with the processes of competitive tendering for a contract for services which will involve the engagement of qualified practitioners, service evaluation and a close accountability for expenditure.

Seventh, in response to the growing complexity of the governance and management of charitable organisations, that management has become a specialism in its own right. In many charities the volunteer 'organiser' has been replaced by a salaried manager and administrative staff.

The consequence of these changes is that there has been a convergence in the nature of the organisational contexts of counsellors working in commercial, public sector and voluntary settings. Today, the counsellors in each of those settings commonly claim or aspire to full professional status, with all that that implies in terms of professional discipline and responsibilities, and in their working relationships with others. Differences remain, but they are not as fundamental in nature as they once were. Significantly, the activities of professional bodies such as BACP have done much in recent years to foster the exchange of information and thinking about good practice between the sectors. In a real sense the content of this chapter is an extension of that dialogue, one in which those in the voluntary sector play a respected role.

Validated knowledge

Other chapters in this book deal in detail with a sharply defined aspect of counselling in community and voluntary settings. This chapter has a title which links every aspect of the enterprise. In framing its content, an effort has been made to demonstrate that the community ventures concerned are not simply 'of the people and for the people' in superficial respects. They are nodes in the community's psychic life in which both catharsis and collusion can occur. As such they encounter influences which can result in them becoming places of greater and more intractable deprivation than that in their communities. Alternatively, they can become models of patterns of mutual nurture which are capable of inspiring the community. Their internal cultures and their effectiveness in their declared roles – sources of mental health care – hinge on the expertise and professionalism of their staff. Here 'staff' is used in its inclusive sense: trustees, managers, appointment secretaries, supervisors and counsellors.

Role differentiation is a classic characteristic of complex organisations and offers many benefits, but the influences referred to above, originating in the community and in the staff themselves, are no respecters of roles.

Trustees and appointment secretaries can be as influential as counsellors in 'collusions to deny'. Those involved in casework, supervision, administrative functions, management and governance need to be alert to the impact that involvement in clients' intimate affairs can have in all those areas and need to function in the closest collaboration. Mutual nurture is a most demanding aspiration. It cannot be achieved in organisational settings where 'them and us' is the organising principle, or where counsellors have supervision, managers and trustees are expected to 'cope', and supervisors' only form of support is external. Experience suggests that the effectiveness of a venture hinges on its capacity to function inclusively, internally as well as externally.

The specifics of clinical practice, supervision and management will continue to be the focus of standard setting, evaluation and innovation. There appears to be every reason to believe that debate will continue about the relative merits of the different theoretical approaches to counselling, the different philosophies of supervision, and the various schools of management. Good in themselves, those processes will fail counselling in community and voluntary settings if attention is not also given to the means by which what Sutherland calls 'validated knowledge' is used to inform the organisation, collaboration and mutual nurturing of those engaged in that work.

'If you aren't mad when you join us you will be by the end of the week!' The community would be impoverished if that quip, made half-jokingly in the past, actually reflected the organisational context in which counselling services are being delivered.

References

British Association for Counselling and Psychotherapy (BACP) (1984) *Code of Ethics and Practice for Counsellors*, Rugby: BACP.
—— (1990) *Code of Ethics and Practice for Counsellors*, Rugby: BACP.
—— (1993) *Code of Ethics and Practice for Counsellors*, Rugby: BACP.
—— (1996a) *Code of Ethics and Practice for Counsellors*, Rugby: BACP.
—— (1996b) *Code of Ethics and Practice for Supervisors of Counsellors*, Rugby: BACP.
—— (1998) *Code of Ethics and Practice for Counsellors*, Rugby: BACP.
—— (2002) *Ethical Framework for Good Practice in Counselling and Psychotherapy*, Rugby: BACP.
Brown, A. (1984) *Consultation: An Aid to Successful Social Work.* London: Heinemann.
Cooper, J. and Lewis, J. (1995) *Who Can I Talk To?* London: Hodder and Stoughton.

Davis, R. and Hill, D. (1995) 'Relate: the changing face of a British voluntary organisation', *Indian Journal of Social Work*, 56, 1: 63–72.

Dryden, W., Horton, I. and Mearns, D. (1995) *Issues in Professional Counsellor Training*, London: Cassell.

Hawkins, P. and Shohet, R. (1989) *Supervision in the Helping Professions*, Milton Keynes: Open University Press.

Hill, D. (1999) '"Hidden groups" revealed', *Counselling Matters*, Rugby: BACP.

Holloway, E. and Carroll, M. (1999) *Training Counselling Supervisors*, London: Sage.

Hughes, L. and Pengelly, P. (1997) *Staff Supervision in a Turbulent Environment*, London: Jessica Kingsley Publishers.

Lawton, H. (1983) 'The myth of altruism', *Journal of Psychohistory* 10, 3: 389–95.

Lewis, J., Clark, D. and Morgan, D. (1992) *Whom God Hath Joined Together*, London: Tavistock/Routledge.

Mattinson, J. (1975) *The Reflection Process in Casework Supervision*, London: Institute of Marital Studies: Tavistock Institute of Human Relations.

Middleman, R. and Rhodes, G. (1980) 'Teaching the practice of supervision', *Journal of Education for Social Work* 16: 51–9.

Searles, H.F. (1986) 'The informational value of the supervisor's emotional experiences', in H. F. Searles *Collected Papers on Schizophrenia and Related Subjects*, London: Maresfield.

Skynner, R. (1989) *Institutes and How to Survive Them*. London: Methuen.

Sutherland, J. D. (1980) *The Psychodynamic Image of Man*, Aberdeen: Aberdeen University Press.

Woodhouse, D. and Pengelly, P. (1991) *Anxiety and the Dynamics of Collaboration*, Aberdeen: Aberdeen University Press.

Chapter 4

Research: the impetus for, and the measure of good practice

A case study from the voluntary sector

Linda Machin

This chapter uses the example of a voluntary bereavement counselling agency – Bereavement Care in North Staffordshire – to demonstrate the dynamic link between research and practice. Four themes will be used to examine this topic:

1   The role of research in service delivery – counselling and therapy.
2   The role of research in the establishment and growth of a voluntary organisation – Bereavement Care.
3   The organisational agendas created by a commitment to research.
4   Two examples of research and their relationship to practice.

Role of research in service delivery – counselling and therapy

Traditionally there has been a divide between researchers and practitioners: the former having an academic concern to understand and analyse phenomena; the latter desiring direct participation with people and their experience. It is perhaps as qualitative research has begun to have an academic credibility and the activities of research and practice have come closer to using similar tools of engagement with their subjects that more practitioners have seen the purpose of research. McLeod (1993) identifies a wide range of areas which link research with practice:

*   elements which may relate to the concerns of an individual practitioner, e.g. letting colleagues know about particular interesting cases or innovations;
*   issues of concern to an organisation, e.g. demonstrating to a funding agency the effectiveness of the service being offered;

- things of broader professional concern, e.g. testing the validity of theory.

However, the unifying theme is that research can no longer be seen as separate from or marginal to practice. Whether it is the exploration of theory, the techniques of practice or the organisational concerns of service delivery, research has a role to play. Standards set by professional groups, training institutions, funding bodies, public 'watchdog' organisations and service users all demand that practice be based upon assured quality. Such assurance is seen in contemporary professional settings as evidence-based practice in which the efficacy and competence of therapeutic intervention is thoroughly tested, and the conclusions used to provide demonstrable guides to good practice. The investigative, enquiring and testing activities of research provide the partnership necessary to ensure that practice is competently, appropriately and ethically undertaken.

This is the rationale for the research focus of Bereavement Care and the research interests span the following areas:

- to help identify and develop service initiatives and developments;
- to inform counselling practice and help to enhance and improve the service to clients (to ensure the service remains needs led);
- to help inform and develop training both internal and external to the organisation;
- to help raise public awareness of the issues relating to death, dying, loss and bereavement;
- to attract funding (from other organisations, through the delivery of training to external organisations, and professionals through publications);
- to enhance the credibility of the organisation, locally, nationally and internationally (which is particularly important within the current climate of competition for contracts, professionalisation of the voluntary sector and increasing emphasis put on research from external organisations such as the Health Service);
- to help facilitate the professional development of paid and voluntary practitioners within the organisation (which in turn aids the overall achievement of research objectives);
- to involve service users and the bereaved/people with life-threatening illness in influencing developments.

Bereavement Care has set out the broad remit within which its research activity will be carried out.

Role of research in the establishment and growth of a voluntary organisation – Bereavement Care

Bereavement Care is an independent charity based in North Staffordshire, UK (not part of the national organisation Cruse). It was established as the result of a demonstrated need which was evidenced by a piece of research undertaken by the author in 1980. The intention of this study was to discover, from personal accounts of bereavement, something of the emotional and social experiences of grief and to explore the mechanisms of support that facilitate (or not) the mourning process. The North Staffordshire area provided a varied social context in which to look at a range of bereavement experiences and 97 people from five parishes participated. This was a quantitative study using questionnaires, which were administered by research assistants. Qualitative data was recorded, based upon additional information given by the respondents and on the comments made by the interviewers.

Indications about the way in which people made supportive use of relationships came from the assessment made by the interviewers based on the interactions within the interview and the reported account of the respondent's engagement within their social network. A general pattern emerged in which those people who had most difficulty in talking about their bereavement were those who were reported to have adjusted least well. For others the benefits of sharing their experience in the context of the study (which was welcomed and appreciated by many respondents) undoubtedly contributed to the view they expressed about the usefulness of talking about their loss.

In looking at expressed need and possible sources of help, 58.8 per cent were thought to have some unmet needs in their bereavement. Of these it was deduced from the qualitative data which supported the responses to the questionnaire that more than 80 per cent might benefit from counselling, either as a single form of help or in conjunction with other kinds of support such as groups, befriending, etc.

The research also demonstrated the wide-ranging ways in which people react to loss. Embracing this difference into a conceptual framework provided impetus for further research. This will be examined in the fourth section of this chapter. Three practical consequences arose from this research:

1   Dissemination of the findings and raising awareness about the need for action in support of the bereaved.

2   The development of a training resource to equip volunteers in care of the bereaved.
3   The possibility of a new care service for bereaved people within the North Staffordshire community.

The first consequence, dissemination of the results, was undertaken through a public lecture and seminars, press releases and publication of the study findings (Machin 1980).

Second, taking the learning forward in order to equip carers, at various levels of intervention, with the knowledge and skill to make effective responses to bereaved people suggested the development of a study programme. Not only would the content of such a course need to be devised, but the process by which people assimilate knowledge and skill in an area overlaid with personally painful material had also to be sensitively acknowledged within the training material. A 'cooperative inquiry group' was formed to look at study design. Participants in this form of research are not so much subjects or respondents but are involved in the dynamic of discovery. The inquiry is an experiential process in which a cycle of reflection and action permits a refinement and critical appraisal of hypotheses and procedures. Reason (1988, cited in McLeod 1999) sees this as a process of:

- initial negotiation about the nature of the research to be undertaken;
- the collection of data using a variety of experiential and qualitative approaches, which process generates a thorough immersion in the subject being studied;
- a reflection upon experience and a re-examination of the original ideas held by the researchers;
- a return to the collection of data newly shaped by the experience and reflection which has started to take place.

Yalom (1980: 153) speaks of the same process but expresses it differently by suggesting: 'Clinical paradigms always emerge intuitively and are justified and validated by their clinical usefulness.'

The author undertook a number of training courses with local volunteers. The material was then produced in a form that could be used with course leaders other than the author and piloted with two separate cooperative inquiry groups: a parish group and a group of volunteer visitors at a hospice. In the light of this experience further modifications were made to the material and the Lichfield diocese then published it in 1983. Subsequent revised and expanded versions were made and *Looking at Loss* was published (Machin 1990).

The evidence from the 1980 survey, of unmet need in bereavement, suggested a service initiative. This was undertaken in 1984 when a pilot project began to look at how a service of care to the bereaved, primarily using a counselling approach, might operate and be resourced. Three important areas had to be considered:

1   The nature of management of the pilot project.
2   The recruitment and training of volunteers.
3   The evaluation of the service.

It seemed important to separate the management function into those issues concerned with the establishment and maintenance of resources and those issues concerned with the competent delivery of service. In the initial pilot stage the important emphasis was upon the nature of the service being offered. Organisational responsibilities were mostly absorbed within the host organisation, the local Citizen's Advice Bureau, and through funding by the Lichfield diocese. A small group of three volunteers was selected on the basis of their pre-existing training as counsellors in other settings. They followed an induction training course, agreed to counsel for one day per week and were committed to ongoing training each month and to fortnightly supervision. At the end of the first six months those who had referred people for support and those clients who had received help were asked to complete a questionnaire. In that initial period 40 clients had been seen and there had been 145 counselling sessions. The sense of 'being safe' and 'being listened to' was typical of the client responses. Criticism centred upon the need to make the service more widely available and more widely known. Referrers also affirmed the support their clients/patients had received and encouraged the development of a permanent service.

At this point the emphasis needed to change to organisational considerations as Bereavement Care moved from its fledgling state to being an independent service. Central to its early objectives was the need for organisational congruence in which both clients and colleagues are valued. These values were incorporated into a statement articulating the 'professional style of the agency' (Machin and Pierce 1996). This identified a core value base in which respect for clients and colleagues would be expressed through non-judgemental attitudes, upholding the right to confidentiality, honouring individuality and difference and ongoing commitment to develop competence and self-awareness.

Evaluation has been an integral part of the process of appraising the counselling and looking at the broader issues of organisational management within Bereavement Care. What became clear is that no single research method addresses the multiple perspectives embraced within the notion of monitoring and evaluation (McLeod 1994). Several approaches have been used by Bereavement Care.

Demographic data

Demographic data derived from agency statistics is a basic and ongoing resource for research. The picture of the number of clients, their gender, age, relationship to the deceased, number of counselling sessions, etc. help to identify the service constituency and its place within wider statutory and voluntary service provision. It also provides information about overt distress and indicates areas of covert need. The trends in service use reflect new specialist provision, i.e. for children as well as the care of adult bereaved. The statistics provide comparative data when looking at other national and international studies on the service needs of the bereaved.

Appraisal of counselling efficacy

Appraising the efficacy of counselling is an implicit part of the supervision function provided for all counsellors within the organisation. McLeod (1994) suggests that counsellors exercise considerable caution in evaluating their own work. However, at the ending of the therapeutic process counsellors are asked to provide an evaluation of their work. Using the tasks of mourning identified within the Worden (1991) model of grief, counsellors are asked to say what the focus of their work has been:

- Focus on the reality of the losses and changes.
- Focus on identifying and expressing feelings.
- Focus on adjusting and reconstructing life as a consequence of loss.
- Focus on internalising memories and ideas of the deceased and redirecting emotional energies.

Assessment of outcomes is made by the counsellors based upon their view of the counselling work and upon evidence/information from the clients. This assessment is completed on a Likert scale and covers the following areas of change/development in the client:

1   The ability to understand and 'normalise' the experience of grief.
2   The overall movement away from emotional vulnerability towards resilience.
3   The overall positive physical/health changes.
4   The overall movement towards appropriate social functioning and/or interpersonal skills.
5   Increasing confidence in own worth and resourcefulness.

The development of client evaluation will be discussed more fully in the fourth section of the chapter.

Action research

Action research arises because each counsellor is moving in an interactive way between their therapeutic role and that of investigator; testing out new ideas and established theories, which in turn shape their practice. As McLeod has pointed out:

> Research is a component of all competent practice. It is not possible to be a good counsellor without possessing a spirit of openness to inquiry. Good research in the domain of counselling and psy-chotherapy always exists in an alive dialectic relationship with practice.
>
> (McLeod 1994: 10)

In a voluntary counselling agency the collective forum for testing individual 'discovery' within practice will be supervision and group training sessions. While these aspects of the work may not overtly carry a research function, it is clear that in the process of reflexivity and exploration of the connection between theory and practice, new perspectives will develop. Clearly learning will be shaped by theoretical insights, but together with the experience of the practitioner there is a powerful source of evolving knowledge. Heuristic inquiry (McLeod 1994) based upon immersion in a subject like bereavement through self-reflection and deep engagement with the experience of others is the basis for investigating a phenomenon. The following are examples of dimensions of new learning to emerge from practice at Bereavement Care:

1   The way in which gender and culture affect emotional expression.
2   The connection between earlier experiences of loss and subsequent coping styles.

3   Notions of normality and pathology in grief, contrasting how they are defined medically and the manifestations in counselling practice.
4   The varied constructions of 'meaning' in relation to loss.
5   The identification of counselling approaches and their appropriateness to particular categories of grief, e.g. children, people with learning difficulties, etc.
6   Methods of facilitating learning about grief in professionals who are involved with people at points of transition and change, e.g. teachers, nurses, etc.

The richness of qualitative learning, which emerges from engaging with the grief of another has provided many opportunities to gain new insight into the nature of grief and the skills needed to respond to it.

Specialist service provision

The organisation has continued to be concerned with the broad areas of need in bereavement but has also identified particular categories, which deserve specialist service provision:

* work with grieving children and young people;
* pre-bereavement work, in support of dying people, those facing life-threatening illness and their carers;
* work with people with a learning disability.

Piloting, that is small-scale, time-limited, fully assessed work in each of these areas, has focused upon the particular needs of the client group, the practitioner skills required to work effectively with them, procedures for appropriate assessment and the accumulated learning for dissemination to other practitioners (Machin 1993). The work with young people and with those with a learning disability has also included piloting therapeutic materials such as pictures, booklets, etc. Work is in progress with the learning disability specialism to produce a practitioner manual to assist in the consistent and confident therapeutic engagement with clients.

Nine small-scale, individual studies have been undertaken for Masters qualifications, for example, a study of parents of murdered children: 'The Meaning of Guilt. A Counsellor's Perspective' (Machin and Pierce 1996).

In 1995 a Research Forum was formed as a new organisational grouping. This was established to decide priorities, strategies and protocols for good research practice. Additionally it provided a setting in which research projects could be shaped and shared within a research culture.

Organisational agendas created by a commitment to research

From the outset, the organisation has based its decisions for the direction and nature of services on a process of piloting. This provides testing of small-scale activity within a reflective process. Informed consideration can be given to the appropriateness of a new piece of work within the human and financial resources capacity of the organisation. Such evidence-based practice has had the benefit not only of providing a strong rationale for practice but also an important justification when seeking external funds. Within the contemporary culture of service provision all voluntary organisations need to be alert to their capacity to provide evidence of the efficacy of their work.

As more people have carried out research within the organisation, a policy has become essential to prioritise the focus and extent of the work to be undertaken. The Research Forum has become the gatekeeper of research and produced guidelines for undertaking ethical research which embody the following central principles:

1   All research should be carried out in a way which maintains the ethos of Bereavement Care; ensuring the rights and needs of clients, non-clients and counsellors as central, whether they are direct research participants or not.
2   Checks on the research aims and methods should be monitored throughout the research process.
3   The design of the research should be consistent with the counselling needs, where clients are the subjects of the research.
4   Clients, non-clients and counsellors who are the subject of research should have their rights and needs safeguarded.

This research protocol articulates the links and interconnections between the counselling function and the research commitment within Bereavement Care. It has made explicit what has always been implicit: that good practice and research are functionally related. Research, like practice, needs to be managed and therefore involves time and commitment for strategic planning.

Two examples of research and relationship to practice

The following examples show the two major dimensions in which research is pertinent to a bereavement counselling agency. First, it is a way of understanding more about the phenomenon of bereavement. Second, it is a way of evaluating practice. In both of these examples the clients are the source of expertise from which the organisation is learning.

Response to bereavement

The focus of this piece of research, undertaken by the author, was an examination of the varied reactions made in response to bereavement. The idea had first been generated by the research undertaken in 1980. A conceptual framework used to categorise the 'Range of Response to Loss', which emerged from that study, seemed justified by practice experience but further systematic research was needed.

The framework proposes that early messages shape the child's concept of how loss and change are managed. These messages are located both in direct verbal information which the child hears from parents and teachers and other messages transmitted culturally via the observable practices and behaviours of the people who inhabit the child's world, together with other influences, e.g. the media. How these messages become internalised will depend upon the child's experience of relationships and life events. The process of combining the message with the experience will produce an assumption about the nature of loss and change, and one's own resourcefulness in response to it. A response to loss is based, therefore, upon an acquired view of the world and 'my' place within it. The process of acquiring and interpreting experience fit with a number of theoretical propositions, e.g. Bowlby's (1980) 'internal working model'; Parkes's (1993) 'assumptive world' and Marris's (1974) 'structure of meaning'. Within the framework, proposed by the author, there broadly appears to be a three category pattern:

1   A response characterised by a view that loss is overwhelming: Loss is emotionally and socially disruptive and the personal and social resources do not adequately militate against its immobilising impact.
2   A response at the other end of the spectrum that seeks to control loss events and the affective consequences: emotional implications are minimised and coping strategies maximised.

3   A third response reflects an ability to achieve some balance by confronting the negative elements of loss and by appraising the positive aspects within a situation, in the knowledge of inner resourcefulness and social support.

The research objective was to design a measure, which might verify the proposed categorical differences and would then identify the grief characteristics associated with each category. A sample of bereaved people seeking counselling help at Bereavement Care was used. A new measure was devised that encapsulated the three different coping styles within statements which demonstrated a personal attitude to loss. This was piloted with 120 undergraduate students and verified within the current study using factor analysis. Profiles of the three categories within the framework were then developed by examining the correlation between independent variables such as gender, age, relationship to the deceased, etc. and dependent variables like the Beck Depression Inventory (Beck and Steer 1984) and the Impact of Event Scale (Horowitz *et al*. 1979).

Having used a sample of people seeking support in their bereavement, it is not surprising that more people featured in the 'overwhelmed' group than in the other two categories of response. Further research looking at a more general population is indicated.

This study using quantitative and qualitative methods was exploring diversity in grief and is therefore important for a counselling agency offering support to a wide range of people. Discovering something about the qualities of that diversity may help in the selection of appropriate counselling approaches (Stroebe 1992–3).

Feedback

The development of a feedback system was seen as a way of testing assumptions about the service being offered to clients, in particular finding out the existing areas of good practice and discovering areas needing improvement (Machin and Pierce 1996). The nature of the research instrument and protocol for collecting the data need to consider the means by which the most truthful answer and the most informative answer could be obtained. Where practice implications follow from data it is especially important to have specific feedback about the experience of the agency and the service it offers. The process used to acquire a multidimensional perspective on the experience of using Bereavement Care included a protocol of covering letters (and the means of ensuring confidential replies) and four questionnaires, which were administered as follows:

1 'Beginning' – this first questionnaire was given to clients after their initial counselling session. The first part of the feedback was requested on organisational issues: initial reception on making the telephone referral; the waiting list; the 'welcome' on arriving at the centre; the centre as an environment; other comments. The second part of the feedback concerned the counselling: five aspects of the relationship with the counsellor were recorded on a five-point Likert scale. Clients were asked to identify both the 'best and the worst thing' about the session and any other comments about the initial experience of counselling.

2 'Ending' – this focused solely on the counselling: the reason for the ending of counselling; what the experience of counselling was like; any alternative preference of counsellor, e.g. age, gender, etc.; length and frequency of the sessions; the most 'helpful and the most hindering' thing the counsellor did; other comments about the experience.

3 Feedback from clients who failed to keep their initial appointment.

4 Feedback where the counselling ended unexpectedly i.e. unplanned.

Although questionnaires were used, the responses were largely qualitative. They had been designed to 'get some sense of the client's story' in relation to their experience of the agency and its service. It was easy to administer and appears to generate a high response rate. Its limitation is the dependence on literacy, which excludes some clients (Machin and Pierce 1996). This has been adopted for general use in the agency and has been subject to some minor modifications.

Conclusion

The nature of many voluntary agencies has changed considerably in the last two decades from a quasi-formal offer of informal services to professional practice, distinguished only from statutory services by the nature of its use of unpaid workers and its funding. Two consequences of this shift towards professionalism have been the scrutiny given to the needs of the client groups being served and the processes of help giving.

This chapter has presented a case study of a voluntary agency and the parallel development of research and practice. The practical rationale for its inception emerged from a piece of research. Throughout its development it has both initiated further research projects, to enhance the delivery of service to clients and to increase the expertise in offering training facilities, and encouraged individual researchers to use the service as host for their investigations. The role of research within the practice setting is justified as a means of furthering knowledge and competent practice. This has made its own demands upon the organisation in terms of appropriate management of research, particularly with reference to ethical standards, and in setting priorities for its pursuit alongside a busy service with limited resources. The foundation of a Research Forum has not only provided an internal base from which to manage research, but has also given it a reference point for the wider networks of academic study and research. This makes many organisational demands but seems an appropriate goal for good quality care in the local community.

The emphasis given to research by Bereavement Care may not reflect the perspective in many voluntary organisations (and indeed, since 2000, the managers of this organisation have chosen a path that no longer gives a place to research). However, this organisational case study shows how the function and methodological diversity in research can effectively serve the needs of a voluntary service and its clients. It could be replicated in many situations.

References

Beck, A.T. and Steer, R.A. (1984) 'Internal consistencies of the original and revised Beck Depression Inventory', *Journal of Clinical Psychology* 40: 1365–76.

Bowlby, J. (1980) *Attachment and Loss, Vol. 3: Loss, Sadness and Depression*, New York: Basic Books.

Horowitz, M., Wilner, N. and Alvarez, W. (1979) 'Impact of Events Scale: a measure of subjective stress', *Psychosomatic Medicine* 41, 3: 209–18.

Machin, L. (1980) 'Living with loss', (unpublished research report).

—— (1990) *Looking at Loss*, London: Longman.

—— (1993) *Working with Young People in Loss Situations*, London: Longman.

Machin, L. and Pierce, G. (1996) *Research: A Route to Good Practice*, Keele: Keele University, Centre for Counselling Studies.

McLeod, J. (1993) *An Introduction to Counselling*, Buckingham: Open University Press.

—— (1994) *Doing Counselling Research*, London: Sage.

—— (1999) *Practitioner Research in Counselling*, London: Sage.

Marris, P. (1974) *Loss and Change*, London: Routledge.

Parkes, C.M. (1993) 'Bereavement as a psychosocial transition: processes of adaptation to change', in M.S. Stroebe, W. Stroebe and R.O. Hansson (eds) *Handbook of Bereavement*, New York: Cambridge University Press.

Stroebe, M. (1992–3) 'Coping with bereavement: a review of the grief work hypothesis', *Omega*, 26: 19–42.

Worden, J.W. (1991) *Grief Counselling and Grief Therapy*, London: Tavistock/Routledge.

Yalom, I.D. (1980) *Existential Psychotherapy*, New York: Basic Books.

Chapter 5

Focusing on the frame

Researching the impact of third parties when working with children

Ela O'Farrell

Introduction

This chapter explores how counsellors working with children experience the wider involvement of parents and other third parties. It summarises a small-scale piece of qualitative research within a local voluntary agency, which looked at how such factors impacted on the intended aim of providing a secure therapeutic frame for direct work with the child.

Data was generated within three focus groups based on reconstituted agency supervision groups and provided insight into the clinical and broader agency issues posed. In particular the research highlighted the significant impact that issues such as fee management, information management, questions regarding child autonomy and maintenance of neutrality posed for counsellors and how this impacted on their management of the secure frame. Agency policies and procedures influenced and reflected the issues posed. The process of research within such an agency, where the researcher was herself employed, raised further parallel issues. Findings resulted in proposals to provide a more secure frame for the counsellor who is acting as container for the wider system of which the child is a part.

Background to the study

The impetus behind this study lay in the researcher's current counselling and past social work experiences of working with children and their families. In both, children frequently experience multiple therapeutic encounters with a range of professionals and carers. These are arranged and facilitated by various third parties, who may be parents, other relatives, foster and residential carers and other professionals such as teachers, health visitors and social workers. These children may live in troubled or disintegrating families or apart from them in foster or residential care. The degree of containment, security or stability has often been limited. A secure therapeutic frame could be a rare opportunity for a stable, safe, regular experience, but in practice is influenced, to a greater or lesser degree, by third parties who are generally the impetus and authority behind the initiation of counselling for the child. It is the impact of this third party involvement that was the subject of this study.

The agency context

The research was conducted in a voluntary family counselling agency, a registered charity, set up to deal with problems causing stress to any family member/s. At the point of research the agency had three branches and 15 counsellors, with another branch due to open. Referrals came mainly from parents responding to publicity or advised to seek counselling by other professionals, most frequently GPs and health visitors. A family centre also made referrals of existing clients. Self-referrals by a child or adolescent were not accepted without adult involvement.

Following an initial assessment, generally with adult family members, decisions were made about the focus of counsellor involvement. Counselling was then offered to the parent/carer(s), the child or adolescent or separate counselling offered to both. An agency contract outlined the purpose of counselling, confidentiality and exceptions to it, duration of sessions and the fee (payable to the agency) and the requirement of counsellor supervision. When working with the child there was a policy of periodic review or check-in meetings with the parent/carer(s), with the child involved in considering the content and their attendance. The duration of involvement was generally according to need.

Counsellors came from a variety of professional backgrounds and theoretical persuasions although all counsellors were female and white. They worked on a voluntary basis, charging a negotiated fee, which contributed to agency costs. Weekly group supervision was provided and group supervisors received their own supervision from an external consultant. Theoretical orientations were not intentionally matched.

The theory context

The psychoanalytic notion of 'the frame' has received significant attention elsewhere (Langs 1977, 1979, 1982; Smith 1991). However, a brief overview and some reflection will serve to provide the theoretical context for this study. The metaphor of the picture frame was suggested (Milner 1952) to identify the boundary setting function of the therapeutic setting. This may comprise a suitable room and its contents, regular times and duration of sessions. Winnicott (1975, 1986) compared the therapeutic relationship to maternal holding where the child can feel safe enough within the established frame to allow the holding and resolution of mixed experiences. The counsellor creates and preserves a space by keeping the external world at bay but also in perspective.

The degree of frame adherence that is desirable has attracted some debate, from being the 'single most powerful factor in the psychoanalytic situation' (Smith 1991: 68) to being a 'phobic concern' (Clarkson 1995: 46). Contemporarily, a degree of flexibility is promoted by House (1999), Lees (1997) and Brown (1994), while Smith (1999: 43) provides the vivid analogy of 'holding the dance' to denote some flexibility of movement. However a useful distinction is provided by Gutheil and Gabbard (1993) between boundary crossing and boundary violation – the former involving stepping out of the usual framework but in a non-exploitative or harmful way, contrary to the latter. In addition to considerations raised for the individual counsellor, the debate also extends to the relevance of frame boundaries within organisational contexts (Jones *et al.* 1994).

Counsellors attempt in varying degrees to establish a secure frame. Psychodynamically, frame ruptures can reflect overt or subconscious messages, which might be accessed through an exploration of the transference and countertransference in a search for their meaning. Psychoanalytic case studies provide vivid examples in work with children. Freud's Dora (1905) was 'brought along' to analysis and on termination Freud commented 'it is only your father who makes you come'. Dolto's 'Dominique' (1974), was similarly taken to therapy by his mother who had the initial interview with Madame Dolto and paid for his treatment (while Dominique waited). The boy was later disturbed by the analyst's awareness of information about himself, which he had not given and she did not explain. In both instances, the third parties to the analysis, the father and the mother, impact on the frame of the analysis by being symbolically present.

So in such third party referrals issues of power and control are significant. How often is it the child's 'choice whether or not to participate in counselling' (BAC 1996: 2.2.12)? Daws (1986) develops this theme, illustrating the complexity of issues of consent in child psychotherapy, and refers to the work of Anthony (1968) who identified how children internalise their parents, their anxieties, ambivalence and conflicting wishes with regard to therapy. Other psychodynamic texts concerning working with children, such as Copley and Forryan (1987), Trowell and Bower (1995) and the more eclectic Geldard and Geldard (1997), typify a lack of detail given to such questions. For example, while there is reference to the need for a dependable time and place for the work, the child's limited control over arrival times etc. is not explored. Geldard and Geldard's reasonable suggestion of making parents feel welcome and valued is undeveloped in terms of the child's possible fantasies of collusion, particularly when parenting is in question. Copley and Forryan (1987) suggest that third party information should be used for 'information only', and yet the impact on the counsellor can be profound. Preparation for and management of progress reports, which are challenging in terms of confidentiality and exclusivity of the counsellor–child relationship, is neglected.

In summary 'the frame', while more or less strictly adhered to, has a strong and continuing tradition in therapeutic work. In relation to children, the inevitable involvement of third parties has significant implications. The possible resulting frame infringements are however less likely to cause 'frame violations' where the interconnections between the parties involved are sufficiently understood, acknowledged and taken account of.

The Research

Methodology

As the theme of the research was the subjective experiences of counsellors, a qualitative methodology was applied. Although focus groups have tended to reflect a more positivist approach, there is some evidence of their relevance within an interpretative paradigm (Barbour and Kitzinger 1999; Secker *et al.* 1995). Focus groups have been found to be 'invaluable for examining how knowledge, ideas, story telling, self presentation and linguistic exchanges operate within a given cultural context' (Barbour and Kitzinger 1999: 5). Such context, both organisational and related to the research procedure, formed the context and part of the subject matter of the study.

Permission to proceed with the research was gained through the agency management committee. An invitation was then extended to all 15 agency counsellors to participate in one of three one-hour focus groups, based on the existing three agency supervision groups. In all, ten counsellors ultimately participated in the study comprising a 'purposeful' (Krueger 1998: 70) or 'information rich' (Patton 1990) sample. Of these, eight described themselves as predominantly person-centred, although five indicated an integrative disposition, and TA and psychosynthesis were also identified as approaches used.

The researcher's own membership of one of the supervision groups was a crucial factor in the conduct of the research and in the analysis. The relative merits and dangers of 'insider' focus groups have been documented (Baker and Hinton 1999). While accessibility, acceptability and awareness of the context were clear advantages, issues of role clarity, dangers of subjectivity and intra-agency dynamics required acknowledgement and accounting for both within the focus groups and in the analysis.

The usual practice of engaging an assistant moderator was not followed due to the small size of the groups and the wish to secure maximum trust, sensitivity and openness while exploring counsellor practice. To improve reliability, this disadvantage was addressed through some oral summary in the groups, electronic recording and full verbatim transcription. Additionally, all initial impressions, highlights and contrasts with earlier groups were promptly recorded and examined. A draft summary of the findings was sent to a participant from each group and telephone comment invited.

A brief schedule of focus questions was devised which, despite initial piloting, was adjusted after the first group to a more open-ended, phenomenologically orientated approach to facilitate more natural group interaction: 'The primary issue is to generate data which give an authentic insight into people's experiences' (Silverman 1993: 91). Electronic recordings, transcripts and researcher notes were scrutinised and key ideas and phenomena recorded and then coded. In view of the more open-ended approach in the latter two groups, a process of axial coding (Strauss and Corbin 1990: 61–47, 94–115) allowed the data to be reassembled in different ways, which resulted in the reported findings.

Findings

General

In each of the three focus groups, the desirability of a safe, intimate, holding environment to enable the child to explore their difficulties was unanimously considered ideal. The age of the child emerged as a significant variable in considering the nature and extent of third party involvement and the feasibility and degree of child autonomy. The boundary between childhood and adolescence emerged as being 12 years of age. The logistics of working with children required contact with third parties at a number of different points in the work and was either managed by another counsellor working with the parent/carer or personally, through correspondence or by telephone. Key occasions were the child's introduction to their counsellor, at reviews, when changes in arrangements were required and at termination. Further key findings are now briefly summarised.

Direct experience of third party involvement

Child autonomy and arrangements for counselling

In each group the child's right to be consulted and involved in each stage of the counselling in an age appropriate manner was a basic assumption. Nonetheless there were clear examples of a reluctance to come to therapy. There was a child who 'came because they wanted her to rather than *she* wanted to come'. Another said 'he doesn't want to come any more because the father was totally against him coming' – this being one of a number of instances of divergent third party views about the child having counselling. In this case the father was 'totally against . . . the child seeing a stranger when he *has* parents'. Even before engagement, counsellors referred to instances where they considered the child was denied counselling due to third party agendas.

Informal telephone contact, ostensibly regarding arrangements, formed a potential infringement of the frame and counsellors referred to their caution in entering into wider discussions. However, it was in relation to termination that a major finding emerged. Here, there were a number of instances of counselling being terminated by the third party, so much so that it was remarked: 'One thing that is striking me is the number of cases we have produced, where the impact of parents ends the counselling for the child.' In one instance a young boy's counselling was ended by his grandparents, who were 'retired and struggling financially and found it a strain coming every week'. The counsellor was told 'we shan't be bringing him any more' and, despite the suggestion of an ending session, the boy was not brought again.

Fee payment

An agency contract specifies the fee agreed with the parent for counselling. Some counsellors however experienced considerable ambivalence in relation to payment for child clients. One respondent felt that parents expected counselling for children to be free, a view reflected in another group with relief that 'at least *we* don't get the money'. A graphic example is the 'fat boy' referred to by one counsellor whose mother would have significantly 'gone without food' to pay for his counselling, who was protected from seeing the payment being made because he worried about it. This reflected the 'bad air' feel about payment for a child where exchange of money was often done subtly, with uncertainty as to whether the child was aware of it. The child was sometimes experienced as passive and uncomprehending in these transactions as if 'they hadn't registered'. One counsellor expressed the view that it was 'potentially complicated' and impacts on the privacy of the work, of the private space between the child and the counsellor. Significantly, fee payment is often a rare point of contact with the adult, sometimes experienced as an unwelcome one, raising the expectancy of some communication or feedback.

Information holding

A significant finding related to the dissonance felt by those counsellors in receipt of information which could not be shared with the other party. This may be due to confidentiality, uncertainty about whether the other party knows or discomfort about invasion of the child's privacy. Various metaphors were used, such as 'leaving issues outside the door' and 'in suspension' or 'in a hanging basket' to symbolise the commitment to compartmentalising such potential infringements to the therapeutic boundary. Nonetheless concerns were expressed about 'maintaining neutrality' and divided loyalties, highlighting the importance of super-vision to manage this. A notable further dilemma emerged where different counsellors worked with each party, where information, maybe contrary to that divulged by the child, was gleaned within group supervision. While some counsellors experienced this as enhanced holding for the child, others saw it as problematic and needing a facility to keep this out of the direct frame of involvement with the child.

Counsellor neutrality

Throughout the research, references were made to issues regarding maintaining neutrality and a non-judgemental stance with regard to some third parties. One counsellor referred to supervision picking up on the 'parental pain', whereas she herself in the work with the child had been 'judgemental . . . to me he [meaning the father] had been the baddie'. Another, in her meeting with parents, found it hard to 'come back to a neutral position and allow them to have their say without seeing it through the child's eyes at that point'.

Concurrently, a key statement drew attention to another dimension of the counsellor's view of the third party. This relates to internal scripts, which might impact on this contact: 'I'm very careful with parents because I think what I would have felt in their shoes.' There was further identification with the parents and acknowledgement of their needs, suggesting that they might 'like to be a fly on the wall ' and 'it takes a lot of courage by parents to bring them'. So the third party, even when making no direct contact, can be very much in the mind of the counsellor. The likelihood of parental fantasies about the role of the counsellor were widely acknowledged: for instance, 'that a stranger is going to come into their son's life and put the son against the father'. It was considered reasonable that a responsible adult would want to know what happens in the counselling and yet privacy for the child makes this complicated.

Some anxiety and irritation with the third party and their expectations of explanations and results in the work with the child also emerged. One counsellor referred to the perceived parental wish that the child's counsellor should 'wave a magic wand' and experienced pressure on her work with the child when 'every week they would be coming and saying "how's X doing?"'

Organisational issues

Assessment processes

The assessment procedure in the agency generally involved a number of sessions with the relevant adults before the child was seen. Nonetheless, counsellors indicated that they worked with what arose in the work with the child, which may not correspond with what was earlier identified as the child's needs. Who defined the need and the goals was a complex issue with an obvious bearing on the later check-in/review sessions. Since indications were that counsellors experienced pressure from third parties to achieve results with the child, the review session could embody an uncomfortable duality if the child counsellor is concerned with maintaining the frame of their work with the child.

Reviews

Reviews legitimately bring third parties into the frame and, in view of the shortage of rooms, physically and psychologically into the child's counselling room. They were experienced as complex events where the frame could easily be compromised. Generally, agreement was reached with the child as to what was to be shared and this could be empowering for the child. Remaining within these boundaries was however a challenge. It was reported that parental material unrelated to the current work with the child may be introduced and need processing or the child may be pitched into role behaviour, not evident in their relationship with the counsellor, which could erode their sense of autonomy.

There were also instances where the child did not want the agreed review and to insist seemed to erode the child's safety. This ambivalence seemed at times to be mirrored by the counsellor: 'I think if the parents are excluded completely . . . and they have the power . . . if they feel they don't know what is going on . . . they'll just give up and not come here any more.' Ultimately a fundamental dilemma was experienced between the desirability of the parent having useful information and the wish to empower the child and maintain the frame.

Supervision arrangements

Here a different source of third party impact emerged – that of the group supervisor's own external supervisor. Two clear instances were described where the counsellor felt the impact in her work with the child of an agenda that had not initially been her own or even coming from the supervision group. One commented: 'You think you're doing one thing and then it comes back that you've got to be doing something else . . . and that makes me very confused.' A particular twist occurred where following consultation with an external supervisor an agency decision was taken to withdraw counselling to a young girl who was refusing to go to school, unless the parents also came to counselling. The refusal ended the counselling to the girl, whom the counsellor felt had been benefiting. Thus, potential breaches of the frame take on a multiple air, with this last counsellor suggesting that 'there's sometimes the child, the parent, us, the supervisor and the supervisor's supervisor' somewhere within the frame.

Parallel aspects in the research process

The exclusion of supervisors from the focus groups produced an interesting dynamic. This occurred following two sessions, when supervisors arrived for the usual supervision session. In one case a sense of exclusion was acknowledged and shared with the group. In the other, interest in group attendance and in the research in general were expressed. In both cases, the groups were anxious to assure the supervisors that they were welcomed back into the group.

A further point of interest occurred in one group with the arrival at two different points of a counsellor and the supervisor. Both offered to wait the final 5 minutes until the group ended but were assured they were welcome to enter. In planning the research, attempts were made to ensure a secure frame for counsellors to participate as openly as possible. Both counsellors and supervisors received explanation of the reasons for the methodology. In the instances outlined, re-entry into the room raised third party issues, which mirror those of the counsellor working with the child. The ambivalence and uncertainties experienced in such situations can be considerable, involving significant emotive forces.

Discussion

In summary, this study explored third party impact in three areas. First, the direct experiences of these counsellors confirmed the challenging nature of such contact. There was consistent reference to concerns about breaching confidentiality, compromising the child's autonomy and invading the child's therapeutic space. Counsellor identification with the parental role as well as experiences of third party pressure impacted on the counsellors. Power issues emerged consistently as having an impact on the boundaries of the work.

Second, the study raised organisational issues, where the organisation itself as the frame or container for the counsellor becomes of parallel significance. Three organisational procedures emerged as having particular impact. The *assessment process* initially was with the third party. As the work with the child proceeded, other priorities sometimes emerged which differed from third party expectations. Following on from this, with the third party 'split off' from the work with the child, opportunities for misunderstanding and fantasy are intensified. Where there is no other counsellor fulfilling the holding function and where the child's counsellor is concerned about maintaining the therapeutic frame with the child, *review meetings* hold the potential for further confusion. Here the counsellor needs to feel within a secure frame. Finally, third party issues are significantly enacted and mirrored within agency arrangements for *supervision*. The examples given point to the significance of the external supervisor's role and how this impacted on the counsellor's sense of autonomy, trust and sense of boundaries in the work – a mirror perhaps of the experiences of the child.

Third, a further indicator of third party impact emerged through the research process itself with the group supervisors' re-entry into the group rooms. While there was some concern over maintaining the frame of the research process, other important realities had a bearing. This would seem to reflect findings in individual adult counselling, where initial frame breaches may first manifest themselves 'between the chair and the door' (Simon 1995) when the session appears over. The need to preserve/not damage the third party relationship and an intuition as to how they may be feeling conflicted with the desirability or feasibility of strict frame adherence, a reflection perhaps of what may occur on arrival of the child's parent or carer.

These three sets of findings, looked at from a psychodynamic perspective, suggest potential for substantial unconscious processes. Some examples will illustrate the point. Monger (1998) has explored how management of fee payment can be a powerful expression of the counsellor's own countertransference issues, where ambivalent and unresolved feelings may be held about money and payment. In a voluntary agency where the payment does not go to the counsellor, further complex emotions are introduced. The situation becomes ever more complex where the client is a child and the payment requires direct contact with a third party and consequent anxieties about the frame of the work with the child. Another example concerns the notion of a non-contractual transference relationship (Clarkson 1995: 54) where the counsellor may experience anxiety about third party misinterpretation of their role, perhaps fantasising about the parental role being usurped. Splitting off the work with the child and the third party relationship may compound such fantasies.

A final illustration concerns the conflicting feelings that parents and carers may bring – such as a conscious wish for the work to succeed but a subconscious hope of failure as a defence against feelings of inadequacy. They may hope for a 'magic wand solution' and indeed the counsellor may carry this through projective identification, ultimately experiencing disappointment with herself and irritation with the demanding third party.

Implications for practice

Since third party impact was found to be inevitable, it must be accounted for. Personal reflexivity and exploration of these issues through supervision and openness to how this may subtly undermine the frame are clearly central.

The agency 'administrative contract' (Sills 1997: 11–45), which establishes the therapeutic frame, could be the vehicle to clarify roles in this three-cornered relationship in the following ways:

1   Specify how changes to arrangements are made and with whom.
2   Identify who pays for the counselling and how and when. This would acknowledge the contractual nature of the relationship.
3   Define the purpose, practice and participation in reviews.
4   Specify the procedure for terminating counselling and agreement to have a final session to acknowledge the ending, as has been suggested elsewhere (Tudor 1999).
5   Supply a copy of the contract in appropriate language for the child.

Reviews provide the opportunity to facilitate and support the counselling process and to maintain change. This study identified a marked reluctance for contact with third parties by the child counsellor. This would suggest the need for a co-counsellor to work with, attend reviews and symbolically 'hold' the relevant adults while child counselling is ongoing. Ideally the review may be held in another room to protect the physical frame of the child's counselling.

While proposals are made to clarify boundaries, it was evident in each group that counsellors valued the degree of flexibility which was possible in this particular voluntary agency. It may be that excessively inflexible boundaries could be counterproductive. Indeed it can be argued that Lang's (1977, 1979, 1982) position in focusing on the external boundaries of the work almost forgets the position of the therapist as the container and the need to maintain those internal boundaries. Thus Smith's analogy of 'holding the dance' (1999: 43) may be an apt one, allowing the counsellor some flexibility for movement in a situation where some third party impact is inevitable, but where the key boundary limitations are made clear.

Implications for future research

This study focused on the child counsellor's experiences of third party contact and how, from their perspective, this impacted on the frame of their work with the child. Further research might develop this picture to include the experience and viewpoint of the child. In the light of suggestions in this study that counsellors are prone to underestimate the child's awareness and understanding of unconscious processes, such research would be particularly pertinent. Indeed, if empowerment and autonomy are to be valid ethical stances in work with children, it would logically follow that their experiences should be heard.

Strong conscious and unconscious processes have been suggested in relation to third party experiences of the child counselling situation. Whether the third party is the natural parent, other carer or a professional, research into the complexity of feelings, fantasies and experiences of those third parties would provide further insight into this complex three-way relationship.

The use of focus groups in the field of counselling research is minimal. This research represents an attempt to adapt the method to a particular context and subject matter and suggests that its neglect in counselling research literature is ill-founded and that there is potential for its further appropriate development.

Conclusion

This study has shown the inevitability and complexity of third party impact on counsellors working with children. By accounting for this impact, the safe frame can be better managed for the work to proceed. Where, as in this study, the counsellor works for an agency, its procedures and supervisory arrangements can be enhanced to provide a safe holding frame for the counsellor, the child and those parties concerned with the child. Such structures are also significant in the work of other professionals working therapeutically with children, in health, education and social services, and it may be that this study also has implications for them.

Acknowledgements

This study would not have been possible without the support of the agency, in which it is based. Thanks are extended to members of the management committee, group supervisors and in particular to counsellors who participated in the research groups and those who subsequently commented on draft summaries. My thanks are also due to my academic supervisor, Dr Lesley Caldwell.

References

Anthony, J. (1968) 'Other people's children', in R. Tod *Children in Care*, London: Longman.

Baker, R. and Hinton, R. (1999) 'Do focus groups facilitate meaningful participation in social research?', in R. Barbour and J. Kitzinger (eds) *Developing Focus Group Research*, London: Sage.

Barbour, R.S. and Kitzinger, J. (1999) *Developing Focus Group Research. Politics, Theory and Practice*. London: Sage.

British Association for Counselling (BAC) (1996) *Code of Ethics and Practice for Counsellors*, Rugby: BACP.

Brown, L.S. (1994) 'Boundaries in feminist therapy: a conceptual formulation', *Women and Therapy* 15: 29–38.

Clarkson, P. (1995) *The Therapeutic Relationship*, London: Whurr.

Copley, B. and Forryan, B. (1987) *Therapeutic Work with Children and Young People*, London: Cassell.

Daws, D. (1986) 'Consent in child psychotherapy: the conflicts for child patients, parents and professionals', *Journal of Child Psychotherapy* 12, 1: 103–11.

Dolto, F. (1974) *Dominique*, London: Souvenir Press.

Freud, S. (1905) 'Case histories 1, Dora and Little Hans', A. Richards (ed.) (1977) *The Penguin Freud Library*, vol. 8, Harmondsworth: Penguin.

—— (1911–1914) *Papers on Technique (Collected Works Vol. X11)*, London: Institute of Psycho-analysis and Hogarth Press.

Geldard, K. and Geldard, D. (1997) *Counselling Children: A Practical Introduction*, London: Sage.

Gutheil, T. and Gabbard, G. (1993) 'The context of boundaries in clinical practices: theoretical and risk management dimensions', *American Journal of Psychiatry* 150, 2: 409–14.

House, R. (1999) 'The culture of general practice and the therapeutic frame', in J. Lees (ed.) *Clinical Counselling in Primary Care*, London: Routledge.

Jones, H., Murphy, A., Neaman, G., Tollemache, R. and Vasserman, D. (1994) 'Psychotherapy and counselling in a GP practice: making use of the setting', *British Journal of Psychotherapy* 10: 543–51.

Krueger, R.A. (1998) *Analyzing and Reporting Focus Group Research*, London: Sage.

Langs, R. (1977) 'Psychoanalytic situation: the framework', in B. Wolman (ed.) *International Encyclopaedia of Psychiatry, Psychology, Psychoanalysis and Neurology*, New York: Aesculapius.

—— (1979) *The Therapeutic Environment*, London: Jason Aronson.

—— (1982) *Psychotherapy: A Basic Text*, New York: Jason Aronson.

—— (1997) 'An approach to counselling in GP surgeries', *Psychodynamic Counselling* 3, 1: 33–48.

Milner, M. (1952) 'Aspects of symbolism in comprehension of the not-self', *International Journal of Psycho-Analysis* 33: 181–95.

Monger, J. (1998) 'The gap between theory and practice – a consideration of the fee', *Psychodynamic Counselling* 4, 1: 36–48.

Patton, M. (1990) *Qualitative Evaluation and Research Methods*, 2nd edn, New York: Sage.

Secker, J., Wimbush, E., Watson, J. and Milburn, K. (1995) 'Qualitative methods in health promotion research: some criteria for quality', *Health Education Journal* 54: 74–87.

Sills, C. (1997) *Contracts in Counselling*, London: Sage.

Silverman, D. (1993) *Interpreting Qualitative Data: Methods for Analysis in Talk, Text and Interraction*, London: Sage.

Simon, R. (1995) 'Treatment of boundary violations: clinical, ethical and legal considerations', *Bulletin of American Academic Psychiatry Law* 20, 3: 269–88.

Smith, D.L. (1991) *Hidden Conversations*, London: Routledge.

Smith, J. (1999) 'Holding the dance: a flexible approach to boundaries in general practice', in J. Lees (ed.) *Clinical Counselling in Primary Care*, London: Routledge.

Strauss, A.L. and Corbin, J. (1990) *Basics of Qualitative Research*, London: Sage.

Trowell, J. and Bower, M. (1995) *The Emotional Needs of Young Children and their Families*, London: Routledge.

Tudor, K. (1999) *Working with the Individual Child in TA Psychotherapy*, London: Sage.

Winnicott, D.W. (1975) *Collected Papers: Through Paediatrics to Psychoanalysis*, London: Hogarth Press.

—— (1980) *The Piggle*, Harmondsworth: Penguin.

—— (1986) *Holding and Interpretation: Fragment of an Analysis*, London: Hogarth Press.

Chapter 6

Assessment for counselling in community and voluntary organisations

Eva Stolte

Introduction

Whilst much is written about assessment for psychodynamic psychotherapy and while psychodynamic counselling trainings refer to this literature (Berger 1999; Coltart 1993; Garelick 1994; Hinshelwood 1991), little if anything is written about assessment for counselling in more general terms. Among several standard readers about counselling, exploring the subject from a variety of angles such as theoretical approaches, settings, themes, etc., assessment is not covered as a topic or even mentioned in the subject index (Dryden 1991). I found one book on assessment for counselling that actually makes the point: 'Some counsellors object to assessment on the grounds that it is harmful to the relationship or to the person (see Rowan 1983: 11–20), or on the grounds that it is inefficient (Dryden 1991), (Ruddell 1997: 16).

Susan Wallbank, writing about counselling in voluntary organisations (1989: 139), points out that counselling was a term first coined by Carl Rogers in the USA in 1942 and his principles of 'unconditional acceptance and respect' were taken up by a wide variety of voluntary organisations who used counselling either as their main or a subsidiary activity in order to help and support individuals, couples or families facing a variety of difficulties. She suggests that with the increasing professionalisation of employees practising counselling and with counsellors able to command proper pay either as employees or in private practice, the community and voluntary sector have come under increasing pressure to compete and to be viewed as just as professional, thus raising expectations of clients as well as funders who wish to see their money put to the best possible use. I would suggest that the interest in assessment for counselling in the community and voluntary sector has arisen in the context of this development. Palmer says: 'Whether we like it or not, our profession does not exist in a plastic bubble, isolated from the demands of society. We are expected to provide a professional service at all times and client assessment is one crucial area of counselling that is often neglected, especially on basic counselling courses' (Palmer and McMahon 1997: 4).

Assessment is part of the professionalisation of counselling and as such can be seen to serve at least two important purposes: first, to make a diagnosis as to what the problem or difficulty is; second, to make a judgement on whether counselling might be beneficial, which might include a kind of prediction as to what approach might be most appropriate and what the duration might be. In other words assessment could be considered as a kind of safeguard for the individual as well as the organisation against unrealistic expectations (on part of the client) and inappropriate requests for help (on the part of the organisation); thus attempting to give both parties the best chance for a positive outcome. Nevertheless this development has also created difficulties in counselling organisations in community and voluntary settings, which will be considered later in the chapter.

Some counselling organisations may adhere to a specific theoretical approach, while others use counsellors from a variety of different trainings and modalities. In this chapter the focus will be not so much on a particular mode or style of assessment and how to do it, but on the importance of assessment and the issues it raises for counselling services in community and voluntary settings. I shall attempt to outline themes and make points which hopefully will be relevant and useful in most settings and to a variety of different theoretical models and approaches. I shall begin with a question.

How does assessment in community and voluntary settings differ from assessment in other settings?

To answer this question, we have to look at the nature of voluntary counselling services in the community. For the purposes of assessment, we could distinguish between two kinds of services:

1   Services that provide counselling for specific problems or difficulties, e.g. rape crisis, alcohol and drugs, victim support, bereavement counselling. These services are usually free and assessment is mainly concerned with making sure the potential client's difficulties are relevant to the service offered. The work is more focused on the particular difficulty and may also be time limited.

2   Services that offer counselling to everyone in the community who seek it and who might benefit. The latter point is an important and not uncontroversial part of the function and purpose of the assessment, but more of this later.

There are some features that all community and voluntary counselling organisations have in common. They are charities that depend on fundraising and therefore have to show that they have a worthy and charitable purpose. This means the service should offer and provide for those most in need or disadvantaged for social or financial reasons. It also means a service largely run and depending on volunteer counsellors, a proportion of whom are students in counselling training. Paid staff are usually limited to assessors and supervisors as most, though by no means all, individuals with the qualifications and experience required for these functions do not or no longer work on a voluntary basis.

Here we may consider several tensions with which the assessors have to contend. To start with, they are bound to the charitable aims of the organisation vis-à-vis the community it serves: in other words to make the services available to as many potential clients as possible. At the same time they have to adhere to their own clinical and ethical judgements and last but not least they have to consider, if not cater for, the counsellors available to take on clients.

Where the organisation is also a training organisation, the assessment is determined by a particular theoretical and clinical approach to counselling. Hence the assessment's focus is on whether or not a potential client is suitable for a particular modality of counselling. The advantage for the assessors is that they can be fairly confident that their theoretical framework and clinical approach are congruent with the training and expected working practice of the counsellors, particularly where supervision is also provided 'in house'. At the same time, they can find themselves under pressure to find potential clients who meet the needs of the organisation, particularly when students need suitable first clients in order to fulfil the requirements of the training. It is difficult to keep an open mind, to stay with the difficulties and needs of the client whilst at the same time being aware that the service already has too many of one sort of client (needing a qualified and experienced counsellor) and not enough of the other (being able to work with a trainee).

Another important part of the assessment (and I will return to this in more detail later) is to give the potential client an idea or a taste of what counselling might entail, a kind of 'introduction to the counselling culture'. Again if the counselling organisation works within one theoretical framework, the assessors can have some confidence in introducing an understanding and a way of working that reflects how, by and large, all of the counsellors in the organisation work. The obvious disadvantage to working within one theoretical frame is the lack of choice. If clients are not considered suitable, or if they do not feel comfortable with a particular approach, the service might not be able to accommodate them.

In my experience as a supervisor of assessors for a psychodynamic counselling service, assessors were very reluctant to deny anyone access to the service on the grounds that they might not be able to benefit from the psychodynamic way of working. There is some flexibility in that 'the psychodynamic way' can be a broad one, encompassing a fairly wide spectrum of styles from the low key supportive to the more intensive interpretative or challenging, with more or less emphasis on the unconscious, or the transference, etc. At the same time, in considering the question of suitability, the assessors often make fairly accurate predictions as to whether someone will take up the referral and how likely or unlikely they are to engage in the process. This could be seen as a kind of do-it-yourself selection, but also as evidence that the service is unable to deliver what it promises to people who are offered counselling. The question here is an ethical one. If the client rejects the service rather than the other way round, it could be interpreted as a 'better' experience because the client, having made the choice him/herself may be keeping a sense of self and hope alive that otherwise might have been injured by rejection. At the same time it has to be argued that it is not entirely honest. But the truth of the assessor's judgement is not necessarily either understandable to the client or without doubt. If in doubt it is only fair to leave the final decision, however conscious or unconscious, to the client. This is illustrated in the following example:

> A young woman came to the assessment appointment with her mother. The assessor explained that she would see the client on her own and the mother agreed to wait. During the assessment the young woman was barely able to speak and initially answered questions in a monosyllabic way. Eventually, with a lot of encouragement, she told the assessor that she had not felt well for some time, had not worked for several years, felt mostly unable to leave the house, did not have any friends, had been admitted to a psychiatric unit on account of feeling suicidal and had now come for counselling because her mother thought that it might help her. The assessor felt that it was imperative that it should be the young woman's decision

whether she wanted counselling or not and gave her some explanation as to what counselling might involve. She asked the young woman to consider this and come back for a second interview. At the same time the assessor asked for the young woman's permission to consult with her psychiatrist. The psychiatrist was consulted and had no objection to counselling.

On the second meeting, the young woman was again accompanied by her mother but she seemed somewhat less shy in the interview, had better eye contact and seemed to convey a sense of hopefulness. She said that she would like to come for counselling. Needless to say the assessor felt that she should be given a chance even though all the indications were that counselling was unlikely to get off the ground, never mind succeed. However, great care was taken to find a counsellor who was willing and might have been able to work with the young woman. The first appointment was cancelled, she attended for the second, but did not return for the third. Her mother then informed the service that her daughter would not attend for any further sessions.

This was obviously not a surprise to anyone, but the question is whether it is fair to offer counselling to someone who is very unlikely to be able to make use of it. Can the experience, however unsatisfactory in terms of service provision and outcome (not to mention time and energy spent), be regarded as positive for the client. One could argue that the failure to establish a good working relationship and achieve any positive change could be detrimental to the client's sense of herself. I would suggest that the young woman's experience of being taken seriously and trusted that she is able to make choices, however limited, may enable her to try again in the future.

Counselling organisations that employ counsellors from a wider variety of training backgrounds have to use a much more open framework for assessment. This presents both risks and opportunities as more clients will be accepted. The risk is that some individuals will prove too difficult or challenging for counsellors to work with. The opportunity, however, might be that counsellors and clients can be matched on a much broader basis. Having said that, in the case of the 'young woman' the particular modality of counselling would have made little if any difference.

The process of assessment

The main aim of an assessment for counselling is to establish whether, and how, a potential client might benefit from counselling. This takes into account what the client brings as well as what the counselling service has to offer. There is no limit to the variety of individuals and their problems but there are limits to what is on offer and this can vary from time to time, depending on the training, experience and availability of volunteer counsellors. The assessment process can be divided into two distinctive functions: screening and assessment interview.

Screening

The screening serves to establish three things:

1   Whether what the potential client's notion of what it is s/he is looking for can actually be offered by the service: for example, marriage difficulties might better be dealt with by an agency like Relate, which offers marital or relationship counselling. Similarly, problems in connection with money, housing, or people with children or relatives with special needs or difficulties, might better be referred to more appropriate agencies. The deciding factor is the potential client's view of their difficulties and his/her expectation as to how they may be resolved or dealt with. In general where advice or practical help or intervention is sought, counselling would not be considered appropriate. If it seems, however, that the potential client is looking for a way better to understand his/her difficulties with whatever the problem might be and hence seeks to find a more satisfactory way for themselves to deal with it, then counselling may be the way forward.

2   The screening process is there to ensure that the agency does not inadvertently take on individuals with difficulties it cannot/is not qualified to manage. People with acute drug and/or alcohol dependency are usually not accepted for counselling. Also individuals with acute or serious psychiatric illness are often not considered suitable, as is true of those who present with serious personality problems.

3   Before a more in-depth assessment is gone into, the potential client needs to know the conditions that the agency requires of the client: i.e. regular weekly time commitment, payment of fees, boundaries around the contact with the counsellor.

Ideally, screening would happen before the assessment in a separate brief interview. In practice some of it may happen in the initial telephone contact, or through sending out of information and questionnaires prior to the assessment interview. Clearly screening will only pick out the most obvious aspects which might indicate that the case is not suitable for the counselling on offer, but I think it is beneficial for the client as well as the service not to raise hopes and expectations which then have to be disappointed.

Assessment interview

The assessment interview can be considered from the point of view of its aim or purpose.

Purpose

1   To establish the presenting problem:

   * long-term or recent onset
   * insight and understanding
   * desired outcome.

2   To explore the ability to make use of the counselling process:

   * Is the client psychologically minded?
   * Is the client able to accept and manage boundaries?
   * What are the client's expectations?

3   To establish the kind of counselling that would be most appropriate and whether the service can provide it:

   * What is the nature of the difficulty?
   * How does the client manage his/her difficulties?

Process

The assessment interview usually takes an hour or an hour and a half and can be considered to have two distinct functions: first, a dialogue about the nature and development of the presenting difficulties; second, gathering of information. These two aspects may form two distinct parts of the interview or may be interwoven. This depends on the style of the assessor, the forms used for the assessment, the time available and, last but not least, on the way the client presents.

Understanding the client's story

The assessment ideally should be a mutual process, giving the client the opportunity to decide whether s/he wants what the service has to offer, as much as enabling the assessor to decide whether and for what kind of counselling the client might be suitable. The client is given the lead in relating his/her story and the assessor appreciates and reflects back how s/he understands the client's difficulties. Some organisations provide a listening service, just for the client to talk over their difficulties. In this process they may get a better understanding of their problem and consequently either decide that they do know how they wish to manage it, or conversely decide that they would want to embark on counselling.

Furthermore the assessor might try an intervention of the kind a counsellor would make in order both to test the client's response, and to give the client an idea of what the work might entail if counselling were to be offered. This can be quite specific where a single shared model of counselling is used, or where several distinctive modes of counselling may be available, but has to remain fairly general and basic if it is to apply to a wider, more generic range of counselling approaches. Ideally in this process potential client and assessor collaborate to come to a shared understanding of the nature and also possibly the origin or source of the difficulties and a tentative view of whether and how counselling might be helpful or beneficial. Ruddell and Curwen (1997) suggest that the way clients perceive their difficulties as well as the way they manage them should be taken into consideration when deciding whether and what kind of counselling might be suitable:

> For example, a person who is totally unable to recognise the interaction of thoughts, feelings and actions will be unlikely to benefit from the cognitive-behavioural therapies if preliminary attempts to orientate the client into the particular framework are unsuccessful. Similarly, a person who is quite unable to recognise the significance of earlier intra-psychic conflict for their current problems, even after the therapist has assisted with this understanding (with interpretations), is unlikely to benefit from psychodynamic therapy.
> (Ruddell and Curwen 1997: 74)

Whilst counselling services in the community and voluntary settings are unlikely to offer a large variety of very distinct modalities, I think that the above example is nevertheless relevant in that it makes an important point: namely, it is very beneficial if not crucial that client and counsellor are reasonably well matched. For this to be successful, it would require the assessors to be quite explicit about the way in which the client may be able to work. Also the person to allocate the case needs to be fairly well acquainted with the way individual counsellors work, not only with regard to using different models or approaches, but also their individual practice.

In this dialogue the client might or might not have divulged a lot of information about him/herself and it is now up to the assessor to make sure that he has all the information required. This information gathering may take place as a distinct, separate part of the interview. If assessing for others, this has the added advantage of putting more distance into the relationship between the client and assessor and thus may facilitate the client accepting that they will not work with the assessor but be referred to someone else. I think that this can be a sensitive issue and it requires skill and confidence on the part of the assessor to engage and then disengage in a way that enables clients to have a valuable experience with the assessor and then make the transition to a new counsellor.

Now the question is what information is relevant and for what. There is information that may be needed to complete the picture. What this means may vary according to the model of counselling on offer, but also depends on what and how the client presents. In other words, assessors need to satisfy themselves that their idea or hypothesis about the client's difficulties and how counselling might or might not work is supported by relevant information. For example, an assessment for psychodynamic counselling would always ask for a fairly detailed personal and family history with an emphasis on childhood and significant early relationships. On the other hand, if a client presents in a way that gives the assessor cause for concern, it is important and justified that the assessor asks for as much information as necessary and possible to get a clearer picture. This may be regarding someone's history of violence, suicide attempts, consumption of alcohol or drugs and, last but not least, previous counselling experience.

In more general terms, information about a person's life circumstances can be useful in providing evidence for the level of functioning. It is useful to know what a person's educational and work history are, whether they have their own support network and what their experience of close relationships has been. To put forward two extremes, a person may present in a state of severe and acute anxiety or distress, apparently unable to cope with anything following some stressful or traumatic event. From the presenting pathology point of view the case may be considered too serious for counselling. Taking into account the individual's history and circumstances, the picture may change to a much brighter outlook if this episode can be seen in the context of someone whose life has functioned well overall, but with an unresolved or denied issue which the stress or trauma has brought back to life and hence led to a kind of breakdown. Counselling could be very beneficial in helping this person to recognise the meaning of his/her crisis and work through whatever the underlying issues are. The other extreme would be a case of someone who presents with a vague feeling of depression, is able to talk about his/her feelings and appears to be very motivated to work hard to find out what is wrong and to get his/her life sorted out. The motivation and enthusiasm have to be seen in the context of the individual's past experience and life circumstances. If those are mostly disappointing, negative and unsatisfactory, it is certainly an uphill struggle, if not unlikely that counselling might prove to be the answer.

In working with clients once a week, whether counselling or psychotherapy, it is vital to establish a good working alliance, particularly working with the 'healthy', functioning aspect of the person. (Bockneck 1991: 183–226). What makes for a good prognosis for using counselling or psychotherapy is good ego function – that is, basic life skills, an ability to distinguish between inner and outer world, an ability to tolerate conflict and an ability to get attached. Conversely, poor coping skills, a blurring of the boundaries between internal and external, no positive attachments and a sense that the problems and difficulties are all coming from the outside world make therapeutic counselling or therapy a very difficult, if not impossible, task.

This also raises the question what kind of counselling might be suitable in terms of time-limited or open-ended work. These options, which could be called therapeutic in the sense of enabling a person to feel and/or function better because of an increased self-understanding and thus an increased choice within recognised limits, are expected to end when either the allotted sessions are done or when both parties feel that enough work has been done. The expectation is that there is a noticeable difference between the before and after. People who might benefit from time-limited counselling have to be able to identify their problem, work on it in a focused way and be able to maintain a good adult working alliance throughout. It is an interesting question whether and in what way assessment for time-limited counselling might need to be different and at what stage the assessor might change tack to explore and test the viability of time-limited work. This question is complicated even further when the potential client comes to be assessed for a limited amount of sessions, often because time and money have been made available by either an employer or an agency making the referral. Does the assessor accept the parameters given? What is the ethical thing to do if time-limited work does not seem to be appropriate? It seems to me that it would only be fair to put the client in the picture as to what may or may not be possible given the limits imposed by the referrer and to explore what if any possibilities there are for further work if needed. With counselling services increasingly open to and competing for contracts to provide counselling for employees of large companies or public services in order to secure a regular income, time-limited counselling is the only viable option. Thus the marketplace, ultimately the employer, rather than clinical judgement determines what is on offer.

Before I go on to talk about the significance of the source of referral, I want to consider the question of supportive counselling. Bearing in mind that a fair proportion of referrals to community and voluntary counselling organisations are people who have difficulties which are longstanding and are affecting them in many aspects of their lives and who also might be recipients of other services, I think that supportive counselling has a significant part to play in enabling individuals to have a better quality of life than they might have without the supportive counselling. Supportive counselling helps individuals to maintain or improve their level of functioning without confronting or challenging their fragile sense of themselves or their views of the world and other people which might be highly coloured by unresolved, early, unconscious, often traumatic experiences. One could also argue that to be listened to and taken seriously in itself can be therapeutic if the client is able to trust the counsellor. What might be considered problematic in offering supportive counselling is that it might create and allow for dependency of the client on the coun- sellor and/or the service. This could mean that counsellors might see one or two of their clients for a number of years, thus slowing down the rate of referral take-up and client throughput, not to mention a drain on often rather limited resources. It also demands a commitment from individual counsellors, which some but by no means all are willing to give. For student and trainee counsellors these clients are largely unsuitable, partly because they do not lend themselves to practise what students are supposed to learn, and partly because in my opinion these clients need to work with experienced counsellors who know and feel comfortable with individuals who require a high level of sensitivity as well as tolerance of high levels of distress and disturbance.

Supportive counselling diminishes the numbers of completed client work and might give the impression that the service is not helping enough people and therefore not worthy of the financial and public support it needs to maintain itself. On the other hand, of course, one could argue that it is exactly those who need the supportive counselling who are the most disadvantaged and therefore most worthy. Another contributing factor to this phenomenon, in my view, is the way that health and social services have rationalised their service provision to be efficient, effective and accountable. Thus individuals whose problems are difficult to identify, who do not fit the criteria, and whose difficulties seem to be of a long standing or chronic nature often do not get any or only very perfunctory help. Many are 'sent' or refer themselves for counselling. One way of identifying people who use the service, which might also be relevant in its evaluation, is the source of the referral.

Referral

The consideration of the source of the referral forms an important part of the assessment. From the patient's point of view, it will tell the assessor something about the individual's motivation. From the service's point of view, it is an indication of where the service is known and how it might be regarded. To put two extreme views:

- The counselling service is seen as a highly selective agency who will only accept well-educated, insightful and articulate people.
- The service is regarded as an open door to anyone who wants an ear to listen.

Obviously a counselling service in the community and voluntary setting would not survive if it was regarded as highly selective, particularly in favour of those who might be able to obtain counselling by their own means from other sources. With regards to the question of motivation, people who have referred themselves can generally be considered to be well motivated, whereas those who have been referred by others may fall into two categories: those who have asked to be referred, e.g. by their GP, social worker, probation officer, etc.; those who have been 'sent' because the referrer thought counselling might be of benefit or simply because they 'should talk to someone else'. Individuals who fall into the latter category may have little motivation and possibly even less idea what counselling involves and this needs to be carefully attended to by the assessor for two reasons. First, it would be for the client's benefit to gain a better understanding of what counselling might entail and how the presenting difficulty might be viewed in this context, as it would enable him/her to make a more informed choice whether s/he wants to take up the service and thus may also increase motivation. Second, from the service's point of view it is important that it is seen by the referring agency as a useful resource with a good reputation for good counselling practice. Therefore, in my opinion, it is important that those who are offered counselling feel able to take it up and make use of it. A high drop-out rate immediately or shortly after the assessment (after two or three sessions) is not only a sign that the assessment is not well managed, but also that the service does not take its work seriously enough, contrary to the belief that by 'providing for everybody' it is doing exactly that. Furthermore it may, of course, create the impression that counselling does not really work and thus be detrimental to the development or even survival of the service.

This leads to the subject of assessment as an important aspect of the evaluation of the service provided. As I said earlier, counselling is subject to increasing professionalisation and is under an obligation to provide evidence for its efficacy by demonstrating that desired outcomes and goals have been achieved. This has significant implications for the assessor and the assessment process in that it shifts the focus from gaining an understanding of the client and his/her difficulty with some sense of what the counselling work might involve and what might be gained, to the need to identify issues and problems which can be resolved. Client and assessor find themselves in an assessment situation which may be heavily influenced if not predetermined by the trend to go for identifiable goals in the shortest time possible. Sutton (in Palmer and McMahon 1997: 171) suggests that 'using a goal attainment approach is both ethical and constructive'. This also provides a way in which outcome can be measured relatively easily. The danger is obvious: If it cannot be proven with research-based evidence, then it is not professional and thus of little or no value. Anecdotal evidence, even if provided as a clinical study within a theoretical framework, is easily dismissed as unreliable. We can all think of some individuals who have benefited tremendously from a modality of counselling or psychotherapy, and others who have not found it helpful at all.

So how does the assessor make a judgement as to what might be of benefit to whom without being trapped into formulating goals that might be attainable in six sessions? Matching seems to be a most significant part of the assessment process in increasing the likelihood of a successful outcome, whether this is measured in numbers of sessions attended, ratings of client satisfaction, or identified goals achieved. A person's predominant mode of functioning may be usefully matched to the counselling modality, i.e. psychodynamic, person-centred, cognitive-behavioural. Tantam refers to research by Royce and Muehlke (1991) who 'found a consistent correspondence between rational therapies and external attributions, and exploratory therapies and internal attributions' (Tantam, in Mace 1995: 22). Other 'matching' factors which appear to have an influence on positive outcome are shared values and similar cultural or religious background (Tantam, in Mace 1995: 9).

Therefore, in my view, assessments can and should be used in the evaluation of the counselling service. To be useful they have to be explicit, not so much as to what the aim or goal of the counselling work might be but how the client might engage in the work, considering the nature of the problem, the history, the relationships and the way in which the story is related, and therefore which kind of counselling or which counsellor might be the most appropriate. A high rate of uptake following assessment is in my view a significant sign that clients' needs are being met and hence of a good service provision.

Conclusion

In this chapter I have raised several issues concerning the assessment for counselling in community and voluntary settings. I have outlined the specific parameters in which assessment takes place and how these may influence the assessment and assessors. In the process of assessment issues arise from the need to screen for individuals who are considered unsuitable for counselling before potential clients are seen for the assessment interview. I hope to have shown that there are tensions between what assessors consider clients need, what the service may be able to provide and, in the case of training organisations and those who provide placements for counselling students, what the service needs in order to fulfil those functions, which have to be managed without compromising in any detrimental way either what is offered to the client or what can be expected from the counsellors who after all provide the service. The aims and the process of assessment are complex and play a most important part in introducing the service to the client, as well as the client to the service.

Assessment and therefore assessors play a crucial role in developing and maintaining a useful and safe counselling service. Whilst needing to appreciate the 'needs of the community', i.e. the source of the referral with its attendant expectations, they also have to safeguard not only the safety but also the professional competence of the counsellors. It can only be in the interest of the client to be offered a service that feels itself to be confident and competent. Only that, I would argue, is what makes a counselling service viable and thus qualifies it for the resources it needs as a charitable organisation.

References

Berger, L. (1999) 'Assessment – the struggle towards objectivity', *Journal of Psychotherapy* 16: 2.

Bockneck, G. (1991) *Ego and Self in Weekly Psychotherapy*, New York: International Universities Press.

Coltart, N. (1993) 'The art of assessment', in N. Coltart *How to Survive as a Psychotherapist*, London: Sheldon Press.

Dryden, W. (1991) *Dryden on Counselling, Vol. 1: Seminal Papers*, London: Whurr.

Feltham, C. (1995) *What is Counselling?*, London: Sage.

Garelick, A. (1994) 'Psychotherapy assessment: theory and practice', *Psychoanalytic Psychotherapy* 8: 101–6.

Hinshelwood, R.D. (1991), 'Psychodynamic formulation in assessment for psychotherapy', *British Journal of Psychotherapy* 8: 2.

Mace, C. (ed.) (1995) *The Art and Science of Assessment in Psychotherapy*, London: Routledge.

Noonan, E. and Spurling, L. (eds) (1992) *The Making of a Counsellor*, London: Routledge.

Palmer, S. and McMahon, G. (eds) (1989) *Handbook of Counselling*, London: Routledge.

Palmer, S. and McMahon, G. (eds) (1997) *Client Assessment*, London: Sage.

Rowan, J. (1983) *The Reality Game: A Guide to Humanistic Counselling and Therapy*, London: Routledge.

Ruddell, P. (1997) 'General assessment issues' in S. Palmer and G. McMahon (eds) *Client Assessment*, London: Sage.

Ruddell, P. and Curwen, B. (1997) 'What type of help' in S. Palmer and G. McMahon (eds) *Client Assessment*, London: Sage.

Tantam, D. (1995) 'Why assess?' in C. Mace (ed.) *The Art and Science of Assessment in Psychotherapy*, London: Routledge.

Wallbank, S. (1989) 'Counselling in voluntary organisations' in S. Palmer and G. McMahon (eds) *Handbook of Counselling*, London: Routledge.

Chapter 7

Issues of containment and holding

Gertrud Mander

Growth of community and voluntary services

From the 1970s onwards there has been an impressive growth in the number of community and voluntary counselling services that has been plausibly explained in terms of the general shift from a religious to a therapeutic climate which happened in the 1960s (Lasch 1979). The churches had lost their monopoly as providers of pastoral care as people turned away from them and the world became increasingly secularised. In their place arose the professions of counselling and psychotherapy which were spearheaded by clergymen and social workers who realised that people's spiritual and emotional needs could no longer be met by traditional methods of preaching, praying and confessing. They adapted theories and methodologies of psychoanalysis, social casework and the humanist gospel of self-help into a form of talking cure in order to assist people with their problems of living (Halmos 1965). The women's movement, sexual and gay liberation and increasing awareness of alcohol and drug addiction among the population led to a gradual specialisation of these services which attracted volunteers and professionals and have since been springing up everywhere in response to widespread demand and need.

I have been involved for two decades in a nationwide network of community centres that have been offering low-cost counselling and counsellor training. United by a common purpose to offer competent and affordable counselling to everybody, the network has grown from rather amateurish beginnings in church settings and village halls to a sizeable professional organisation with sound structures of administration, financing and training whose competent services are sought after, well used and have acquired a reputation for excellence. This is due to well-functioning systems of delivering and evaluating its services which are focused on providing a containing environment to both staff and clientele. By this I mean a place where people feel safe to work and to talk about themselves and, if they are trainees or clients, to learn, grow and explore themselves (Black 1991) in a supportive and facilitating environment.

Holding and containment: the facilitating environment

By using terms like containment, holding and facilitating environment when speaking of organisational management I have been drawing on concepts developed by the analysts Bion (1972) and Winnicott (1960) in the context of child care and human relating in dyads. These have since been widely applied to situations where strong feelings and anxieties need to be 'held together' to enable administrative or clinical activity and organisational growth.

When such language is used, the analysis of community and voluntary organisations such as my own is enriched by a dynamic human dimension. Where people are seen for counselling and are trained in counselling they urgently require the provision of a 'holding environment' like the individual child in order to get on with their complex tasks and to achieve their specific goals and expectations, which always generate anxiety and insecurity. The term 'holding' conjures up the image of a mother's safe embrace, of a protective shield, physical, emotional and symbolic, which offers shelter, safety, rest and comfort to a dependent and growing young creature. It can also be seen as a space for playing, creating and communicating that is firm, flexible and adaptable. As such it is appropriate to transfer the concept from its original domestic context to the open system of a community counselling service where staff and clientele gather and work together as strangers and colleagues performing many different and difficult tasks which require them to feel safe.

The holding environment of which Winnicott speaks is an entirely beneficial stucture: ego-supporting, enabling 'maturational processes', adapting to changes and, more specifically, allowing the effective performance of primary tasks (Menzies Lyth 1988). It needs to be reliable, offering empathic, good enough care and, above all, allowing the managing of intense anxieties and guaranteeing a 'continuity of being' – as to the child, so to the organisation.

We can also think of the system as a container that receives, creates, holds and emits administrators, secretaries, trainers, trainees, clients, etc.

This describes a structure that hums with creative activity, thinking, learning and servicing, management, training, and clinical work, and represents a setting that is expressly designed and maintained for these purposes. In contrast to Winnicott's simple and unified external structure of holding, Bion, to whom we owe the clinical concept of containment (which has since been used in many organisational contexts), distinguished between container and contained, outer and inner, server and served. He described three different forms of the working dyad that he called 'symbiotic', 'commensal' and 'parasitic'.

The first is a relationship where one person depends on the other to their mutual advantage – like child on mother, client on counsellor, customer on organisation. The second is a relationship in which two objects share a third to the advantage of all three – like supervision, the core family, or a small group. The third is a relationship where one depends on another to produce a third, to the destruction of all three – power struggle or rivalry in a family, intrigue or competition in an organisation, sabotage in a task group. The point is that containment, unlike holding, can be both integrating and destructive – a secure base, a distancing strategy, a thick skin, a defence against anxiety. Thus, in the words of Pietroni (1999: 417), it can be 'transformative', represent a 'safety net', or become 'a repressive strategy' that 'sets limits which feel brutal' – always depending on the choice of maternal or managerial style.

In an organisation such as a voluntary agency or community service, the way management handles authority and provides support determines whether there is cooperation or strife, task or anti-task behaviour (Menzies Lyth 1988: 50). Thus it is important whether there is openness or defensiveness among staff and clientele, and also whether there can be creative flexibility rather than rigidity and formality of organisational procedures and back-up systems. Good managerial containment allows the fluctuating collective and individual anxieties to be managed and kept to levels which facilitate the adequate performance of primary tasks.

The voluntary, i.e. largely unprofessional nature of the population, whether administrative, clinical or consumer, makes for an unpredictable climate in which the possibilities of conflict, breakdown or crisis are legion and 'social defences against primitive anxieties', as defined by Menzies Lyth, will easily flourish. This term has been successfully applied to the dynamics in 'human service' organisations ever since the publication of the author's celebrated study of a London teaching hospital, which was commissioned by the Tavistock Institute of Human Relations in 1955 ('The functioning of social systems as a defence against society' in Menzies Lyth 1988: 43). She used Kleinian notions of early defensive structures to describe unconscious organisational behaviour under stress and advocated the analysis of organisational systems in terms of constructive 'containment of anxiety in organisations' that would lead to constructive task behaviour instead of the pedantic anti-task behaviour which she had noticed among the hospital's nursing hierarchy, and identified as the reason for the high drop-out of trainee nurses and the inefficiency of administrative functioning that had occasioned the original request for help.

As I am concerned with a therapeutic organisation I would like to add the concept of 'frame' as helpful in describing the maintenance of purposeful task behaviour in a counselling and community service. The frame has long been considered an important therapeutic tool (Langs 1994). First used by Marion Milner, this term, also known as 'the analytic setting' (Winnicott 1960), indicates a safe and constant framework in which the analytic process evolves, meaning above all the physical, space–time, frequency and rhythm aspects of the work. Winnicott defined the 'setting' as a 'sum of all the details of management that are more or less accepted by all the analysts', in other words, basically a 'mental attitude of the analyst, that sets the scene for action like the darkness in the cinema, the silence in the concert hall' (Flegenheimer 1982). Bleger (1967) takes up the term 'setting' and suggests that we apply it to the totality of the phenomena that are included in the therapeutic relationship: 'those that make up the process (which are what is studied, analysed and interpreted) and the non-process, i.e. the frame – that is, those constant elements in which the process takes place. This constant structure has the same function for the patient as symbiosis with the mother has in the development of the child's ego: it is a support, a framework, that only becomes evident when it breaks down'. For this reason Bleger thinks that the setting can become 'the repository of the most primitive part of personality, the psychotic part'. With this statement Bleger joins hands with Elliott Jaques (1955), who coined the concept of 'social systems as a defence against anxiety', and with Menzies Lyth (1988), who applied this concept in her classic study, written in 1959, about the 'primitive anxiety which nurses experience in their work with hospital patients'. He thus identifies and confirms the need for firm containment which all work in medical and therapeutic contexts requires.

Returning now to my community centre setting, I would like to incorporate firmly this clinical vocabulary in the ongoing analysis of its organisation. When I spoke of the amateurish beginnings to our network I meant the spontaneous initiative and the voluntary offer of help, the provision of a place and a framework in which people would be encouraged to talk freely about themselves and would be listened to attentively and at length. Apart from telling their life stories they could thus explore their emotional difficulties and find solutions to the conflictual life situations in which they felt stuck and overwhelmed.

On the whole, the development of managerial structures and supportive back-up systems came later, as the numbers of staff and service users grew and the clients' need for more sophisticated understanding of their dilemmas became apparent. The helpers would also soon realise that they required responsible ongoing supervision of their cases and to this was added a thorough training in counselling skills, in clinical assessment, an enhancement of self-awareness and the acquisition of clinical concepts to penetrate the complex states of mind, symptoms and behaviour patterns that the clients presented with. In the course of time the helpers and their trainers inevitably discovered the client in themselves and came to realise that they too needed some personal therapy in order to understand their own problems and to separate their conflicts and dilemmas from the feelings the clients projected onto them and constantly burdened them with in the course of therapeutic interaction.

Each of the growing number of community centres went through a similar dynamic development from small beginnings with a charismatic leader and a handful of pioneers through various stages of organisational complexity with increasing numbers of participants performing different roles whose tasks became delegated and separated. Finally they joined together to form a supportive network that had its headquarters in London and its affiliated or associated members in the regions.

Functions of support and administration were split up and subsystems for specialised activities developed, work procedures became codified, clinical and administrative practices were standardised and a bureaucracy became necessary to list, record and classify the mass of data relating to the counselling service, the trainings and the complicated schedules of activities carried out and attended by all the people who worked in or came to the organisation regularly.

The success of an organisation and its temporary or continuing quality of containment depend on the clarity and suitability of the structures created and maintained to perform its functions and services in a harmonious balance of all its parts. A nationwide network of counselling centres like the one I am describing, where there is a requirement to conform in broad outline to the structures, guidelines and systems developed at headquarters over years of experience, can only survive if it consistently offers an environment safe enough for its staff and the service users. It is important that it reliably delivers the standards of efficiency, confidentiality and regularity necessary to keep the tasks and performances going.

The particular quality of containment and holding demanded of a counselling centre, where day in day out troubled people come to receive relief of their emotional pain and to unburden themselves in the privacy of their counsellors' consulting rooms, is a high degree of practical and emotional support for everybody, not only for the clients who expressly seek this out; be it in the form of supervision for the staff and trainees who deliver the counselling, regular staff meetings for the administrators, trainers and technical workers, recurrent reviews and exchange of information relating to changes and forthcoming events, to the financial health of the service and plans for the future. As so many people are part time in such an organisation, an occasional get-together of the whole service or the celebration of a seasonal event will strengthen the sense of belonging and build the solidarity that is the cement of good working relations and high motivation among the staff and the senior management. The latter should always remain visible and available for consultation which will contribute greatly to a general sense of being remembered and appreciated.

Another factor that guarantees a safe holding climate is the balance between openness and confidentiality among the staff with regard to clients and colleagues and the way in which difficult matters such as deaths, resignations, appointments and other personal or personnel changes are handled and communicated. Gossiping in corridors and common rooms is unavoidable, as is a certain level of anxiety when major changes become known. Particularly difficult to contain are financial worries, drops in client numbers or in the recruitment of trainees, resignations, sackings or personality changes at senior management level.

The most unpredictable difficulties are, however, the levels of unconscious anxiety that are brought in or produced by the client population at any time and which cannot be measured or foreseen, only contained with the help of sound structures and healthy defences. When training is going on, there are certain times such as the beginning and end of the year and periods around trainee assessment that produce more anxiety among staff and trainees and require special measures of containment like group reviews, rituals like orientation days or graduation events and written procedures for appeals, grievances and deferrals which allow the channelling and voicing of anxieties.

Twenty years ago, when I first joined a small community centre in the larger network, I was a greenhorn, just qualified, and had to take on a fortnightly supervision group of untrained volunteer counsellors who were keen but very anxious to get it right and needed firm and authoritative holding. I was helping a female colleague run the centre, with the two of us doing everything from counselling, supervising, assessing, selecting counsellors and clients to running workshops, arranging special fund raising and social events and participating in the management committee. This met periodically and consisted of the director, who was minister of the Methodist church whose premises we were allowed to use, the treasurer, a retired civil servant, our administrator, who was a volunteer and one or two counsellors.

We shared the space with a day centre for the elderly, a play group and a youth club, and were struggling to keep the boundaries, to keep the noise levels down to an acceptable level and to train the other users of the church not to barge into our ongoing counselling or supervision sessions. When we were joined by a male social worker who had volunteered to run a supervision group it became glaringly apparent that we did not know much about how to manage and develop a fast-growing organisation, had never troubled about drawing up our terms of reference, to give ourselves a constitution or devise rules of professional conduct. The centre could feel quite unsafe, particularly in the evenings when counsellors sometimes had to work in the dark in an empty building. The need for containment became a pressing priority, from security locks to curtains, to arrangements for receptionists and lockable filing systems. Our colleague's organisational experience helped us devise some simple organisational structures which held the centre together, promptly reduced the anxieties to manageable levels and made it feel professional for the first time.

Unfortunately we two women fell out with each other after a few creative years over the issue of staff meetings, which were demanded regularly by my colleague who had appointed herself to the post of counselling coordinator and asked for my administrative and meeting times to be given free. Her demands for support became more frequent whenever her anxieties increased, and I became resistent to more and more extra tasks because I wanted to concentrate on my clinical work. In the end she decided to introduce a rule for supervisors to be given time-limited contracts of five years, which was exactly the length of time I had served as a supervisor and meant that I had to go before I was ready for it. This could not happen now, but such measures of moving the goalposts were common in organisations where changes were made by individual managers without discussions with staff. They were a form of the 'parasitic' containment which Bion described as potentially quite destructive and liable to produce rigid defences against anxiety such as splitting and denial.

Appraisal

In the beginning the individual centres were relatively autonomous and much of what was going on there was unknown at headquarters. They therefore tended to become incestuous and lax on administrative and clinical boundaries until headquarters decided to institute regular appraisals. These were meant to serve as a monitoring and evaluation device and to be conducted by appraisors from the wider network who were familiar with the common purpose, the administrative systems which had been agreed for the network as a whole and the clinical procedures that were considered necessary to uphold the BAC Code of Ethics and Practice to which the network subscribed.

On the basis of a thorough appraisal, individual centres were granted (or withheld) affiliation to the network which had a common director and a joint council of management. The appraisals became regular events and produced an inspectorate system that was designed to offer supervisory, consultative and developmental help while careful not to arouse suspicion and resistance to being patronised and intruded upon. To some affiliate centres, opening their books felt like exposing themselves to parental disapproval and being questioned as to staffing and clinical procedures, and certainly like not being trusted to do it right. Instead of being a form of commensal containment, this was experienced as parasitic and repressive and produced a demand for greater autonomy within a looser democratic structure. For a while there was a danger of the network breaking apart in this mutinous resistance to a management that was experienced as authoritarian rather than authoritative. The crisis was eventually weathered, but it was characteristic for an organisation which was trying to develop from a paternalistic to a sophisticated democratic managerial structure of interdependence and consensual teamwork.

The first appraisal visits had still been experimental in an attempt at working out an efficient monitoring system and left behind a sense of having been checked and controlled. This was counterproductive as the intention had been to help and advise by making centres look at themselves and being looked at with an expert eye. In time, the appraisors were given a sensitivity training and instructed to work from accurate checklists, write reports to an agreed formula and invite a critical post-appraisal report of the appraisal from the visited centre. This gradually began to feel like being part of a 'commensal' containment event in which the beneficiary was also a partner and the recipient of constructive assistance in their strategic plans for the future.

Development in the network as a whole was moving from the haphazard do-it-yourself methods of the early days towards a structure of interdependence, in which the centres participated voluntarily and agreed democratically to common administrative systems. Recruiting and staffing procedures were coordinated and financial development plans became de rigueur, based on realistic forecasts and the establishment of reserves. In the end the network devised a training and accrediting scheme to replace existing local initiatives by nationwide certificate and diploma courses in counselling skills and counselling training that would enable graduates to work in the centres as staff counsellors or set up private practice in their communities when they had reached the required professional levels. A central training committee approved the individual centres' training submissions, which were pitched at various levels of professionalism. It also monitored trainee assessments and awarded graduate qualifications. Finally a training course for supervisors was set up and held at central headquarters and this offered a diploma in supervision that achieved national and academic accreditation as a Masters degree, providing the network with a steady flow of well-trained supervisors.

Meanwhile, the counselling services for clients on a low-cost basis, the main and original purpose of the network of community centres, were growing apace; now supplying clients for the trainees to practise on rather than being seen by volunteers from the community, as in the beginning. These clients are mostly referred by GPs, psychiatric hospitals and social services, or self-referred through word of mouth; people having picked up leaflets at libraries, attended open days held at the centres, or heard of the service on the community grapevine.

The centres have the full responsibility for their finances and keep going on clients' voluntary contributions, training fees and funds raised from the community, the local authority, charities, or by any other means. The network has also been trying to get funding for special projects, like AIDS or serious physical illness counselling, and it is increasingly trying to establish contracts with GPs, primary care trusts and industry, also offering time-limited work to the corporate sector through employee assistance projects. An effort was made to be included in the NHS outcome research project (CORE) based at the University of Leeds that has resulted in some government funding of the counselling of lower income groups for the network as a whole and will eventually be written up as a research project into the effectiveness of counselling.

The maintenance of high standards of safety and confidentiality is essential for the competent functioning of a counselling service and the network has developed careful systems of reception, assessment, monitoring and bureaucratic recording to contain the input and through-put of large numbers of customers, their personal data, scheduling and matching with counsellors and rooms. Regular allocation meetings, weekly supervision of staff and trainees, a well-functioning appointment system and efficient bureaucratic methods overall constitute the foundations of a database that registers centre users and centre workers in a transparent roster. Gatekeeping through reception staff available during the working hours, round-the-clock telephone services and up-to-date computerisation provide a holding environment for the extensive information needing processing and containment on the premises. Over the years a detailed intake and assessment system has been developed to make sure that all clients have some medical cover, have access to their files if they ask for it, and can receive a psychiatric consultation if there is urgent need for it. They are familiarised with the health and safety procedures and clear lines of accountability and responsibility are established to safeguard their rights and their welfare while they are being treated (Jaques 1976).

The need for the observation of professional boundaries is uppermost in a place where people come for help with sensitive personal issues. This is easier done at headquarters where the premises are spacious, allowing some privacy and the separating of clients from staff, trainees from trainers, whereas the smaller centres up and down the country are handicapped by limited resources, though the general sense of community is more highly developed there. As the network operates within a psychodynamic theoretical orientation, it is pledged to keeping the analytic frame uppermost, honouring Bowlby (1988) for postulating a 'secure base' as fundamental for secure attachment and Langs (1995) for insisting on the priority of the 'secure frame'. Compared to the NHS practice of flexible appointments, with doubling and trebling of bookings to allow for patient dropout and attendance laxness, the appointment rules for clients are clear: start on the hour, finish after 50 minutes to allow for an interval to switch rooms, and observe absolute punctuality and reliability to maximise the sense of containment, support and safety. All this is designed to establish the provision of good enough care, managing anxieties and thereby ensuring the 'continuity of being' of which Winnicott (1960: 52) speaks so eloquently in relation to the holding and facilitating environment.

What finally determines the quality of holding and containment is the style and continuity of management which enables an organisation to go through its inevitable stages of growth and crisis, and which determines the structures of communication, consultation and decision making. During the 30 years of its existence the network has had three directors whose management styles differed widely, while being determined by the climate of the time as much as the individual personalities.

In the beginning there was the founder, a Methodist minister who had received a US training in pastoral counselling and who was an inspired 'shaper' (Black 1991: 89), a mover and shaker whose ability to inspire (and hire) others to help him with his self-appointed task of offering counselling to the multitudes (Freud 1919) was unbounded. He unfortunately burnt himself out while attempting to realise his vision and died suddenly, leaving much work still to be done. This traumatic death rallied the troops behind the widow and the coordinator of counselling. After a brief interregnum in which the institutional anxieties rose to breaking point, a successor was found who boldly took on the task and carried it on in an authoritative rather than authoritarian managerial style. This relied on consensus and team management without paternalism, gradually giving up the founder's pastoral dimension and imaginatively diversifying the training programme in order to improve the precarious finances and move the organisation into a central position in the burgeoning counselling world.

This administrator embodied Ekstein and Wallerstein's ideal administrator (1958: 27): understanding, supportive, sympathetic to therapeutic values and insistent on high professional standards, protective of the 'clinical rhombus' (of administrator–supervisor–counsellor–client) and of the holding environment, equidistant from each and everybody. He possessed the final authority which he used sparingly, and graciously gave up his post on reaching retiring age, leaving some debts but no bad feelings. He worked on consolidating the foundations and also inaugurated some expansion of the growing network of counselling centres as well as the headquarters' activities, which involved some joint research with the psychiatric outpatients of a large teaching hospital as well as pushing initiatives like group work, counselling in companies, training in supervision.

What followed was a directorial regime of less visibility and more unpredictability, at times laissez-faire, at times quite authoritarian, which was in many respects in tune with the big changes in the external world, what with the regulation of the profession, the accreditation of courses and counsellors, the training link-up with a university and the ever-growing financial difficulties which were temporarily stabilised with the help of the corporate monies flowing in through valuable contracts with banks and other businesses. The network was bureaucratically streamlined as much as possible, had acquired an annual conference to strengthen its sense of solidarity and common purpose, and its graduate association was steadily growing. Link-ups with universities and the professional bodies of BACP and UKCP were established for the counselling and psychotherapy trainings and the network's profile became quite well known, though survival anxieties were never far from people's minds.

To illustrate this I want to end with some stories of crisis and intrigue that produced high levels of paranoid anxieties about the future. The first of these involved a training supervisor in an affiliated centre who felt excluded from the assessment of clients, the selection of counsellors and the decision making in the centre and complained about being sidelined. She felt her expertise was not used and too much power was in the hands of one person who took decisions about trainees without consulting her. She was supported by some of her colleagues, but felt not listened to by the decision-makers, and became very angry when a trainee was removed from her supervision group without consulting her. This incident made her hand in her resignation and produced an exodus of training supervisors. It was too late for mediation and the centre shook to its foundations, feeling unsafe for everybody, until a new training coordinator and new supervisors had been found and installed. The importance of validating and including supervisors had been neglected by the management, hence the container had become unsupportive.

Next, the director of a large provincial centre who had moved sideways to devote himself full time to clinical services had become engaged in a rivalrous relationship with the chair of the management committee. Both male and intransigent, they did fierce open battle over every decision and a split developed around them which was noticed and addressed during an appraisal visit. Inevitably, one of them had to go and in the end it was the director who had not been elected like the chair and was self-appointed. The reverberations of this aggression charged power struggle were seriously undermining. It was splitting the organisation and people were leaving in droves, including clients. For quite some time afterwards the place did not feel safe for getting on with the counselling task and fears of sacking persisted.

Voluntary organisations in the counselling field are particularly precarious because they are usually operating on a financial knife-edge, never able to offer enough pay or job security to staff and dealing with vulnerable people. Firm personal boundaries and containing managerial structures with thoughtfully built in back-up support like compulsory supervision and local advisory councils are therefore indispensable for their continued survival and when the managers fail 'things fall apart and the centre does not hold' (W.B. Yeats).

I have been describing the network during a period of steady growth, both of the counselling services and of the counselling psychotherapy and group trainings. More recently, this has slowed down, due to the fierce competition with a plethora of mostly academic new training courses. Hence, an atmosphere of crisis has been developing which has been difficult to contain, as the future looks uncertain and anxieties about losing a big enough share of the market have increased. The competitors are cheaper, offer easier and shorter courses leading to the same qualifications and do not depend on a shrinking revenue from clients. It looks a bit like the bust after a boom which had been so exhilarating and gratifying while it lasted. The recent advent of brief counselling schemes in the corporate and primary care sector has also become a challenge that is difficult to contain, as once again there is a money factor fuelling the competition. Other changes are in the air too, such as the shrinking of the private sector and the fast development of new technologies such as telephone and internet services which will open up opportunities for therapies of all kinds and simplify access to vast numbers of potential clients.

Conclusion

What has happened to counselling after its auspicious and idealistic beginnings just a few decades ago? Where has the charitable community spirit gone that fuelled it at first? Rarely has a profession gone so fast through a cycle of growth, expansion and decline (Mander 1997). Yet hopefully the difficulty is only temporary and new initiatives may soon be found to help us out of the impasse which money issues and a bad press have created. The discovery that many people who did not have a good enough holding and containment in their infancy can be helped to better living by an experience of holding in therapy in a community setting later in life has undoubtedly come to stay, though the forms of delivery and the contexts and settings in which this will happen are going to go on changing.

References

Bion, W.R. (1970) 'Container and contained', in W.R. Bion *Attention and Interpretation*, London: Maresfield.

Black, D. (1991) *A Place for Exploration, The Story of the Westminster Pastoral Foundation, 1969–1990*, London: Westminster Pastoral Foundation.

Bleger, J. (1967) 'Psychoanalysis of the psychoanalytic frame', *International Journal of Psychoanalysis* 48: 511–19.

Bowlby, J. (1988) *A Secure Base: Clinical Applications of Attachment Theory*, London: Routledge.

Ekstein, R. and Wallerstein, R. (1958) *The Teaching and Learning of Psychotherapy*, New York: Basic Books.

Flegenheimer, W.V. (1982) *Techniques of Brief Psychotherapy*, New York: Jason Aronson.

Freud, S. (1919) 'Lines of advance in psycho-analytic therapy', in *Standard Edition: Vol. 17*, London: Hogarth Press.

Halmos, P. (1965) *The Faith of the Counsellors*, London: Constable.

Jaques, E. (1955) 'Social systems as a defence against persecutory and depressive anxiety', in M. Klein, P. Heimann and R. Money-Kyrle (eds) *New Directions in Psychoanalysis*, London: Tavistock.

—— (1976) *A General Theory of Bureaucracy*, London: Heinemann.

Langs, R. (1994) *Doing Supervision and Being Supervised*, London: Karnac Books.

Lasch, C. (1979) *The Culture of Narcissism: American Life in an Age of Diminishing Expectations*, New York: Norton.

Mander, G. (1995) 'In praise of once-weekly work, making a virtue of necessity or treatment of choice?', *British Journal of Psychotherapy* 12: 1.

—— (1997) 'Towards the millenium: the counselling boom', *Counselling* 8: 1.

Menzies Lyth, I. (1988) *Containing Anxiety in Institutions, Selected Essays, Vol. 1*, London: Free Association Books.

Pietroni, M. (1999) 'Containment in theory and practice', *Psychodynamic Counselling* 5, 4: 407–28.

Winnicott, D.W. (1960) 'The theory of the parent–infant relationship', in D.W. Winnicott *Maturational Processes and the Facilitating Environment. Studies in the Theory of Emotional Development*, London: Hogarth Press.

Chapter 8

How does the nature of the client group or the presenting problem affect the clinical work?

Sue Cottrell and Alison Elgar

This chapter will be dealing specifically with the issue of sexuality and asking whether separate counselling services should be available for lesbian or gay clients. We will not be including the issues relevant to bisexual clients although we acknowledge that some of what we discuss is relevant to bisexuality. We will also not be looking at the question of gender in any detail. Lesbian and gay are often put together, yet there are differences between the two, not just in terms of culture but also in terms of gender. This will not be discussed in this chapter. We hope to be raising more questions than we answer and offering food for thought, consideration and reflection, rather than the definitive guide to lesbian and gay specific counselling.

As authors we are committed to the idea of lesbian and gay specific services. However we believe these will not be without their own difficulties. It could be argued that sexuality is inherently about relationships, and it is the therapeutic relationship that concerns and interests us as therapists. The different aspects of working with lesbian and gay clients, as 'out' lesbian therapists, provides much 'grist for the mill'. It is working for lesbian and gay services that proved insights and further explorations not necessarily available within a generic counselling setting. It is the provision of counselling for lesbians and gay men, by lesbians and gay men, within a safe, supportive, non-pathologising environment that forms the basis for healing.

Both authors of this chapter have worked for specialist lesbian and gay counselling services. This work informs our discussion of counselling services for lesbian and gay men, providing services specifically for lesbians and gay men and those questioning their sexuality. We are counsellors and come from different theoretical orientations. What we have in common is the fact that we both positively identify as lesbian.

Generic versus specialised provision

Should separate counselling organisations meet the needs of specific client groups, or does generic counselling have more to offer? Does generic counselling more effectively meet their needs? The answer to this seems to depend on whom you ask. There is certainly much current debate which we will discuss here. Our informal research amongst lesbians and gay men indicates that most would prefer a gay or lesbian counsellor, yet Spinelli suggests that in some circumstances, for example, if the client wants to break cultural taboos, it may be better that the therapist comes from outside that culture in order to help the client explore the issue more objectively. The issues are complex and whether or not the therapist's culture matches that of the client, it is clear that the therapist must be able to 'to "be" from a framework of a flexible self-construct' (Spinelli 1994).

Of the lesbian and gay men we spoke to, most are qualified counsellors. This raises a further question as to whether clients who are trained counsellors have different expectations to those who are not. In order to begin discussing this topic, we think it is necessary to highlight the climate in which we write. There is no doubt that we live in a homophobic society. The controversial attempt to repeal Section 28 has highlighted society's fears. There appears to be a fear that children will 'turn into' homosexuals. Little concern is given to those children who are confused by and questioning their sexuality, or who have parents who are lesbian, gay or bisexual. From our experience of counselling lesbian and gay clients, many express having felt bullied at school for being gay or lesbian; and many of these had not themselves recognised or come to terms with their sexuality at that time. The effects of the bullying left many gay adults lacking in confidence and self-esteem. Stonewall (1996) found that 48 per cent of those aged 18 and under had experienced one violent attack, of which 40 per cent took place in or around schools. A survey undertaken by the Institute of Education on behalf of Stonewall reported that '82 per cent of teachers said they were aware of homophobic abuse in schools and 26 per cent said they were aware of violent bullying motivated by homophobia'. Negative homosexual messages absorbed 'can be a wounding experience for the self-esteem for young gays and lesbians. Social isolation and fears for the future are often compounded by lack of information about homosexuality . . . The risk of rejection by family, friends, and peer group is a fearsome one for young people'. This rejection, based on homophobia, leads to many consequences: 'Over-represented among the young homeless, many gays and lesbians are forced to leave home because their families will not accept their sexuality' (Hill 1995). Trenchard and Warren (1993) found that 'of 416 lesbians and gays aged between 15 and 20 years in the London area 19 per cent reported a suicide attempt'. McColl (2000) found that one in five lesbian and gay youths had inflicted serious self-harm more than once and this included serious suicide attempts. Research conducted by the University of Luton, shows that 'bullying and other reinforcements of homophobia promote social and emotional withdrawal, isolation and depression in later life. Additionally, the absence of support from peers and fear of disclosure to parents and teachers and subsequent rejection, further promote feelings of hopelessness and despair, leading to thoughts of self-harm or suicide' (Davies 1996: 135). Research in the USA also supports this evidence (Gibson 1989; Rofes 1990).

Bearing this in mind, many lesbians and gay men are left feeling very threatened and vulnerable. So why would this client group seek counsellors from amongst the heterosexual majority who are seen as the cause of their fear? According to McFarlane's research (1998), most participants felt that having the choice was very important. Developing a specialist service and not improving mainstream organisations was not good enough. The majority of people interviewed wanted a specialist and mainstream service, but a mainstream service that was safe and sensitive. Many however thought that this was a long way off and therefore felt that specialist services were needed until such a time generic services could develop sufficiently. Specialist services were thought necessary because the participants in McFarlane's research did not want to 'be on the receiving end of homophobia and heterosexism'. They were 'more likely to receive empathy, understanding and rapport' from lesbian and gay men counsellors. They would have an 'opportunity to meet people with positive sexual identities' and their sense of 'loneliness and isolation would be reduced' (McFarlane 1998: 106).

The arguments for having specific counselling organisations are manifold. The old debate is raised as to whether someone can counsel a client when they haven't experienced that client's issues or culture. How can a heterosexual counsellor support a client's experience or work through 'coming out'? How can a heterosexual counsellor enter the world of lesbian and gay men clients without any previous knowledge or experience? Many a colleague in training has confessed that they have no problem with homosexuality, and then find difficulty answering the question 'how would you feel if it was your daughter/son?' As Brian Thorne (1990: 115) says: 'No therapist can confidently invite his client to travel further than he has journeyed himself.' For the heterosexual counsellor, understanding and being at ease with homosexuality, like many issues, is a layered process and requires commitment to working with the various issues that come up. We also need to consider the definition of a straight or heterosexual counsellor. We believe that sexual orientation is represented as a continuum and one that has fluidity and is not cast in stone.

Obviously there are many issues that a lesbian or gay male counsellor may not have experienced or come to terms with. How many counsellors, however, are able to recognise a lack of competency before taking on a client? No matter how well informed a counsellor feels about working with gay clients, there is always the issue of unconscious homophobia. The client's process of trying to deal with the counsellor's homophobia, conscious or otherwise, can only detract from the client's presenting issue and the work they are bringing to their sessions.

In this society, the majority of external stimuli relate to a heterosexual life style, advertising, media, government slogans such as 'Victorian values', 'back to basics', 'the pretend family', to name a few. No matter how open minded and judgement free we feel we are, we all have the potential to be unconsciously homophobic. This applies to gay clients and counsellors too, but gay counsellors may be more aware of this issue. Is this a case where empathy is not enough?

In terms of life experience, a gay counsellor has knowledge of living in a heterosexual world, whereas the majority of straight counsellors are not familiar with living in a gay world. Without this, how can someone know what it is like to experience subtle/indirect homophobia, disgust from others about your sexuality, oppression, not knowing whether their disinterest or dislike of you is because of your sexuality or some other reason. Where does a gay client begin to explain these issues so a straight counsellor can begin to understand? Why should a client have to spend the first few sessions, and intermittently throughout the counselling relationship, educating the straight counsellor? Many gay clients spoke of having to explain the language of the gay scene, terms such as cruising, cottaging, bachelor, bull dyke, butch button, which altered the level of the relationship. Some would argue that this is how straight counsellors learn to work with gay clients. How else are they to integrate? Obviously the clients are not there to take on the role of educator; they are there to be served by the counsellor, not the other way round. There is a subtle difference between having to educate the counsellor and the counsellor learning from the patient.

Some straight counsellors, having just started to work with a gay client, begin to realise that they have very little knowledge of homosexuality and by this time have begun to form a therapeutic relationship with the client. We discussed this chapter with some heterosexual counsellor colleagues, after which one began seriously to question her competence in working with a gay client. Does the counsellor decide to stop working with the client, and thereby seemingly reject her/him because of their sexuality? Does the counsellor continue and say nothing, hopefully educate themselves and/or learn from the client, or (depending on the theoretical perspective), discuss it openly with the client? What a position to put the client in. In the case of a decision to refer on, whatever the reason, there is always the possibility that the client may feel very rejected. To a client who may already be feeling extremely vulnerable, depressed or bereaved, whatever their presenting issue, this can only serve to 'damage' their self-esteem and wound them even further. To seek out counselling can be a very difficult process for some; to be rejected, pathologised and not feel heard or understood at the end of it could quite possibly add further distress.

It is our view that non-lesbian and gay counsellors and their clients would benefit from lesbian and gay men awareness training. Most general counselling courses tend to marginalise training sessions on working with lesbian and gay men clients. At best lesbian and gay men issues are included as a short, student-led seminar (which in our experience have often been run by lesbian and gay men and been excellent). At worst this is ignored totally, the argument being that courses cannot include every topic. This leads us back to the question of whether we should or could work with clients we are not trained to work with.

Many gay clients want to work on life issues that may not directly relate to being gay, for example, loss, sexual abuse. However, it could be argued that all life experiences are influenced by the perspective of sexuality. Counsellors can fall into the trap of defining the client by their sexuality and assuming their sexuality to be a problem. This can detract from the presenting issue. Conversely, it is 'vital and essential', as one person exclaimed, that gay clients see a gay counsellor because sexuality can be bound up with many issues such as alcoholism, bereavement, grieving about a dead partner and not being out, or depression about being isolated and humiliated for being gay.

The question of the efficacy of specialist or generic services can also be affected by whether one sees some issues as global, or whether they are gay and lesbian specific. Take a lesbian couple, for example, one of whom is experiencing difficulty living with and integrating her partner's children from a previous relationship (which could have been hetero- sexual or lesbian). Does this circumstance present definite 'lesbian issues' that need addressing by a gay counsellor, or are the underlying themes the same as if the couple were a man and a woman? The question also arises whether the lesbian couple would benefit from a woman/lesbian opposed to a male/gay male counsellor, and does that lesbian counsellor need to have experience as a mother, biological or non-biological?

It has been argued that specialisation makes the issue (in this case homosexuality) 'not normal' and only aids segregation rather than integration within society, and of course can reinforce homophobia. There are other factors that place specialist organisations at a disadvantage: for example, most such organisations are reliant on voluntary sector/charitable funding and are therefore vulnerable to having that funding withdrawn. At times of pressure this makes the organisation not feel unsafe and therefore possibly provides an unstable environment for an already shaky client – thus mirroring the position of minorities in society. The existence of specialist organisations also means that generic establishments are reluctant to improve their attitude towards homosexuality. The focus of attention becomes the client's sexuality, and promotes a ghetto mentality (McFarlane 1998).

A gay counsellor has the advantage of understanding most of the issues brought by the gay client, from a place of knowing universally. Obviously all clients are unique and therefore each experience is unparalleled, whatever the issue, but at least a gay counsellor has the edge. However this can cause complications with the clinical work (see below). On the other hand, a lesbian and gay counsellor has not always experienced the same level of homophobia as the client, for example, or may not have suffered from parental rejection as the client has.

Clients simply do not want to be judged for being gay. Although there has been much research pointing to a rethinking of Freud's claims about the immaturity and narcissism of homosexuality (O'Connor and Ryan 1993), psychoanalytic thought has been and still is used to define homosexuality as a mental illness and consequently something that can be cured. Clark (1987) however adds that counselling theory, even humanistic, cannot be neutral as we are all subjected to societal homophobia. Galgut's research (1999) asked counsellors about working with lesbian clients. Galgut found that 'a number of respondents espoused pathologising attitudes towards lesbians. For example, lesbianism is a result of sexual abuse, nurturing that was negative or a fear of male sexuality'.

Many people we have worked with have felt their sexuality has been pathologised, which leads us to believe that although homosexuality is not classified as a 'mental illness' any more, many professionals do not share this view. The assumption seems to be that non-heterosexual lifestyles are unfulfilling and gay relationships do not last long and are less satisfying. Gay clients want to feel their counsellor is holding the whole picture, and not from a heterosexual perspective. This notion is borne out in relation to supervision of lesbian and gay counsellors. Supervisees have reported that they feel more relaxed and open about their client work in a lesbian and gay organisation compared with a majority heterosexual organisation. They experience the supervision as holding the whole picture.

Many clients we have seen have worked with other therapists or mental health services where their experience has been that their sexuality is viewed at best with incomprehension and at worse as the root of their difficulties. Many lesbian and gay clients have suffered long-term discrimination, have been ostracised from family and rejected by friends. Many may have suffered physical as well as emotional abuse as a result of their sexual orientation. They may experience guilt about their sexuality, and have many negative images internally about themselves and the way they have relationships. Thus their desire is to be understood in some way and (unlike in the heterosexual world) not to have to 'justify' their sexual preference.

We have received clients who have been recommended by their counsellors to go to a specific lesbian and gay men organisation purely to deal with gay issues. We also have knowledge of GP surgeries that have openly admitted that they will not/do not offer gay affirmative counselling. On the one hand this could be seen as the counsellors recognising their limitations and competency (as per the BACP Code of Ethics 1996), or it could be seen as conscious or unconscious homophobia. As with most homophobia, it is sometimes difficult to define as it can be very subtle, and one is left not truly knowing. McFarlane (1998) looked at studies to try and identify the beliefs and attitudes held by doctors towards lesbians and gays. Bhugra (1988) found: 'Ten per cent of GPs think gay patients should be returned to normality by therapy and two thirds feel uncomfortable having gay men as patients.' Rose (1994) found that 'doctors are influenced by the values of their culture and in many instances are blatantly homophobic'.

We believe the therapeutic relationship is paramount to the work. We began to think about what this means for us as practitioners and for our clients. What are the implications of a therapeutic relationship where not only are both client and therapist gay, but also the relationship is conducted within a lesbian and gay counselling service? What are the implications for the counsellors and the supervisors? This unique setting distinguishes this as a specific issue. Regardless of our theoretical influences, in order to work for these services we are seen as lesbian therapists. The choices we may make in private practice as to whether or not to disclose our sexuality are not present at these organisations.

The counselling services we have worked for are in high demand, so much so that often there are quite long waiting lists. People are willing to wait as they want to come to a lesbian and gay counselling service. For many men and women their desire to see a lesbian or gay therapist within a gay setting is the priority. As we have discussed, this desire has many roots. As well as the external factors influencing people's choice to come to a specialist organisation, there are also the deeper therapeutic issues. Through our work we have seen how clients frequently present with an assumption that they are coming to their own 'community', that they will be understood and be with someone who can relate to their experience. In essence, they come with the view that they will be seeing someone who is the same as them. This is understandable if we consider the all too frequent experience of oppression and marginalisation for lesbian and gay men clients. There is a sense of relief for lesbian and gay men clients that they can ask to see a lesbian or gay counsellor and that their sexuality will not be pathologised. There is the knowledge that they can come and talk freely about their intimate relationships without the fear of naming their lover as a woman or man. Many clients report feeling very comfortable, knowing everyone they see positively defines as lesbian or gay.

If this is true for clients, then it will also be 'true' for us as therapists. We too have our own histories of 'coming out', the painful acknowledgement of our different sexuality, experiences both positive and negative with families, friends, neighbours, etc. We too have our own internalised homophobia, feelings about how we see ourselves and our identity in the world. We too will have our own reasons for choosing to work at a lesbian and gay organisation. Like our clients, have we chosen to work somewhere we hope will feel comfortable, somewhere we hope will feel like our own 'community' and where we believe we will be able to understand our clients?

Why do so many clients present with the assumption that they will be 'understood' by a lesbian or gay therapist? What will the impact of this issue be on the therapeutic relationship? Here we must address the issue of loss and grief that frequently arises for clients we see in these settings. These feelings are manifested in a number of different ways. The issue of 'coming out', a phrase that is usually applied to someone who is beginning to name their homosexuality to themselves and/or others, is a common issue that clients present. As we have already said, coming out is often a very painful journey for someone to embark on. We live in a homophobic society. We are surrounded by images of what it is to be loved, to be accepted, to be happy, to be rich, to be good, to be 'normal', and these images are overwhelmingly heterosexual. Thus to begin to name our 'otherness' through acknowledging our sexuality is to question most of the assumptions that we would have been brought up with and which we would have lived our lives by.

Naming ourselves as gay has profound repercussions. The very act of 'coming out' is to name ourselves as different, as other than the majority of society. After all, how many heterosexuals 'come out'? The assumption is that we are all heterosexual unless we name ourselves as different. To name ourselves as lesbian or gay can be experienced as a relief. Many report that they had reached a point where they felt they had to come out as they were living two lives, an outer acceptable life in society (at work, with family, etc.) and a private 'real' life as gay. Many feel an increasing need to bring the two parts of their lives together and come out in every area of their lives.

Thus 'coming out' can bring a sense of power, of relief, of unity, but it can also be accompanied by a sense of loss. Naming one's sexuality as different brings with it the loss of our idea of ourselves as taught by society and family. Thus if I am gay, then I am not heterosexual. If I am not heterosexual then where do I fit into this society? What is my idea of myself if the self I thought I was I have now discovered to be false? In addition, if I am no longer heterosexual and thus no longer part of society as a whole, then presumably I cannot be loved, accepted, happy, rich, good or 'normal'.

All too often 'coming out' does indeed include very concrete losses. Many experience rejection by family, friends, colleagues, etc. Thus naming one's sexuality is very clearly associated with a sense of bewilderment, isolation and confusion. But on a more profound level, coming out also brings feelings of confusion when clients begin to look at who they are now that they have named their difference. It is this existential crisis that causes some to look for a safe place to replace the world they thought they knew. So coming to a lesbian and gay organisation can feel a replacement, fuelling the need for a organisation or family who will not reject them.

The community of the heterosexual world, despite its difficulties for some, can be a hard community to be rejected from when it is often the only safe and secure place people have known. So there is a need to replace this with something else when the crisis of coming out is upon you. The need to replace the lost community with another, the need to feel held and contained, is profound and often what clients are looking for. The expectation is that if they come to a specific service they will find the safety, the understanding, the containing, the confirmation of identity that they have lost and need to rebuild.

The idea of the crisis of identity ties in with Winnicott's (1970) idea of the need for the mother to be good enough, to mirror the child's needs, desires, expressions, so as to allow the child to internalise the mother's good sense of herself, integrate it and in time discover their own sense of themselves. In some ways, this may be what is happening when clients come for counselling in a state of crisis over their identity. They are looking for the safety of 'good enough' (Winnicott 1970: 190) mothering from the face of the new community. Their sense of themselves is very shaky and they are looking to have their new sense of self mirrored, reinforced and internalised.

So even before clients come, there is an 'agency transference' set up in terms of their expectations and hopes from this new community. Yet is this what actually happens for clients when they start counselling? Sometimes what happens is that clients can get extremely disappointed. They are confronted neither with the mirroring that they desired, nor the accommodation that they had expected their new community to give them. Rather they are confronted with the limits of what the agency can do, and the disappointment of working with someone whom they discover, although being lesbian or gay, is in fact different from them. Some clients begin to find this rejecting and punishing, and experience it as not meeting their needs. They are let down by their families and let down by the organisation. This experience of coming out and the subsequent loss and disappointment can touch on their early damaged object relations.

If we work on the assumption that for both therapist and client there may be very similar motivations for being at a lesbian and gay organisation, then for both of us there may be an unconscious drive for collusion and over-identification. If the outside world has been experienced as discriminatory and persecutory, then the desire for comfort, to be known by the other, to feel 'at home', to be understood and to understand will be very strong. If we have been hearing from our clients their distress and pain, often specifically related to their sexuality, is there a danger that we will collude in an attempt to make everything better for them, rather than challenge and question as we may another client who is more obviously different from us? For to question the client's experiences will mean that we will question our own, however painful that may be for us.

Additionally, there may be a danger that we will assume we know what it is the client is talking about because we both share similar experiences. Thus in some way our curiosity and desire to know what it is like for that other person may be dulled. An example of this is a client Y seen for short-term work at a lesbian and gay service. Y was a woman who had grown up in eastern Europe, but she had similar life experiences to the therapist. Y felt she had been quite damaged by her relationships (with both men and women), particularly as a younger woman, while involved in an isolated political movement. Her experience of 'coming out' within what she now viewed as a suffocating environment had damaged her a great deal. She had suffered abuse, particularly at the hands of women whom she felt had sought to control her with little thought for her feelings or growth as a young lesbian. She would describe her experiences and often punctuate it with 'you know what I mean'. Although the counsellor's and client's experiences were in some ways very different, there was sufficient mutual experience and the counsellor felt she knew what the client was describing.

The work felt very 'stuck' until the counsellor began to realise that she had been assuming she knew what it was like for her client. As she began to realise what was happening the counsellor began to be more curious about her experiences. What was it like for her client during those years? What had drawn her to become involved in this particular movement? What had caused her to move away from it to the point where she now looked back and felt it had been 'suffocating'? What did it mean for her now to choose to come to a lesbian counselling service and request to see a lesbian counsellor?

In terms of the relationship these enquiries had an enormous impact on the client. Both had been working on the assumption that each knew what the other was speaking of. To question this meant that Y had to discover what it really meant for her without reference to what her counsellor may think or feel. More importantly, it raised the issue of how it was for her to be working with a woman who she knew to be a lesbian. Her experience of being controlled, told what to think, how to behave, etc. had on an unconscious level been recreated through the therapeutic relationship; a relationship that was also being conducted within a separatist environment. The counsellor had not queried what it had felt like for her, thus not truly leaving her the emotional space to think about and try to understand what it had been like for her and what she was left with.

The counsellor's realisation and subsequent change in approach with Y initially left her feeling very angry. The lack of curiosity had meant that for her she had developed a false sense of security with the counsellor (as she had as a young woman within a movement which she felt had promised her a great deal of security and a sense of family, but which had not lived up to its promises). She talked of feeling angry with the counsellor as she felt as though what had happened between them had been similar to her previous experiences. The counsellor's over-identification had left little room to explore her differences and had conveyed to her that maybe the counsellor also could not tolerate the differences between them.

When these differences began to be named it caused her a lot of pain and distress. She began to feel the pain and bewilderment of being different; feelings she had sought to erase. So it was a double-edged sword. She had wanted to be understood, after all she had come to a lesbian and gay counselling service, had requested a lesbian therapist. She had wanted someone who was like her in order for her to feel as though she was being understood. Yet the very act of collusion and over-identification between them only served to reinforce for her the pain of her past experiences, leaving her fettered to her own fear of being different.

Connected to the idea of over-identification between client and therapist – desiring to be understood connected to choosing to come to a separatist organisation – are the expectations which are set up. As stated before, many clients attend with the unconscious notion that they will be understood, will be embraced by the organisation and in some ways that all their needs will be met. This is reinforced by the organisation as it gives clients many options as to who they can see (e.g. choose the gender and ethnicity of the counsellor), thereby setting up a situation where the promise of needs being met is present even before the clients attend for counselling. In addition, the very existence of the organisation is built on the premise that other therapeutic services have failed lesbians and gay men in some way by not truly understanding or accepting their sexuality.

Although on one level this is true, on another level it seems to set up an expectation that the therapist will be able to meet all the client's needs. As in all therapeutic relationships, the issue of transference and countertransference plays an important role. This is particularly pertinent if the therapist works, as we do, with the therapeutic relationship as central. There is a specific dynamic set up when the client knows of the therapist's sexuality. So this combination of an agency which promises a great deal, with therapists disclosing their sexuality, can sometimes have quite profound implications for the transference and countertransference, as highlighted by the case study above.

Conclusion

In conclusion therefore the answer to the question of whether a specific or generic organisation meets the needs of lesbians and gay men, is not straightforward enough to merit a yes or no response. Some lesbian and gay clients want lesbian and gay specific services and some do not. Others feel that they do not have confidence in 'gay friendly' or generic services. It would be ideal if we could depend on and trust generic services, but unfortunately we do not live in an ideal world. Hopefully this chapter has helped the reader to reflect on the complexity of factors to be considered when attempting to answer this question. We hope to have encouraged awareness of some of the issues for both therapist and client when attempting to deal with the dilemmas raised.

References

Bhugra, D. (1988) 'General Practitioner, 15: 2', in L. McFarlane *Diagnosis Homophobic – The Experience of Lesbians and Gay Men and Bisexuals in the Mental Health Services*, London: PACE.

British Association for Counselling and Psychotherapy (BACP) (1996) *Code of Ethics and Practice for Counsellors*, Rugby: BACP.

Clark, D. (1996) 'The new loving someone gay', in D. Davies and C. Neal (eds) *Pink Therapy*, Buckingham: Open University Press.

Davies, D. (1996) 'Pink therapy: a guide for counsellors and therapists working with lesbian, gay and bisexual clients', in D. Davies and C. Neal (eds) *Pink Therapy*, Buckingham: Open University Press.

Galgut, C. (1999) 'A fair deal for lesbians in therapy – an ethical issue?, *Counselling* October: 285.

Gibson, P. (1989) '*Gay male and Lesbian Youth suicide: Report of the Secretary's Task force on youth suicide. Vol. 3: Prevention and Interventions in Youth Suicide (Alcohol, Drug Abuse and Mental Health Administration)*', London: The Stationery Office.

Hill, K. (1995) *The Long Sleep, Young People and Suicide*, London: Virago.

McColl, P. (2000) 'Report of the GLAM Study, St Edwards Hospital, Cheadle', in A. Mason 'A queer law – what counsellors should know about section 28', *Counselling* April: 138–9.

McFarlane, L. (1998) *Diagnosis Homophobic – The Experience of Lesbians and Gay Men and Bisexuals in the Mental Health Services*, London: PACE.

O'Connor, N. and Ryan, J. (1993) *Wild Desires and Mistaken Identities*, London: Virago.

Rofes, E. (1990) 'Notes on suicide and suicidal ideation among gays and lesbians', in R. Kus (ed.) *Keys to Caring*, Boston: Alyson Publications.

Rose, L. (1994) 'Homophobia amongst doctors', *BMJ* 308: 586–7.

Spinelli, E. (1994) *Demystifying Therapy*, London: Constable.

Stonewall (1996) *Queerbashing*, London: Stonewall.

Thorne, B. (1990) 'Person centred therapy', in W. Dryden *Individual Therapy*, Buckingham: Open University Press.

Trenchard, L. and Warren, H. (2000) 'Something to tell you: London gay teenage group', in A. Mason 'A queer law – what counsellors should know about section 28', *Counselling* April: 138–9.

Winnicott, D.W. (1970) *The Child, the Family and the Outside World*, Harmondsworth: Penguin.

Chapter 9

Putting 'technique' into question

Paul Gordon

> Under the sway of a belief in technique we tend to follow what is considered proper and respectable, what we can report to our colleagues or put into print without seeming naive or irresponsibly reckless. Even more formidable . . . is the dread of appearing to be sententious, sentimental, or pretentious if we try to describe our experience in terms other than that of technique. How can one convey the deep feeling that can be aroused when we manage to reach another's heart?
>
> (Lomas 1994: 74)

Providing counselling or psychotherapy within an organisational setting can bring many benefits to the counsellor or therapist, not least of which is the opportunity to share one's work with colleagues and to learn from their thoughts and experience. Unlike work in private practice which is pretty well closed off from any external scrutiny, work in an organisation is usually open to the scrutiny of colleagues, whether peer colleagues or managers. Over time, such colleagues may get to know each other and their ways of working well and be an invaluable resource of support and friendly advice and criticism when needed. A problem can arise however when an organisation seeks to impose a particular way of working on its counsellors or therapists; a way of working that is usually derived from some firmly held theoretical position that defines the nature of the therapeutic work. In such circumstances, therapeutic work can too often become a technical practice, a matter of following the correct procedures as laid down by the theory in question. In this chapter I want to put this idea of technical practice into question, drawing on my own experience of working therapeutically within organisations.

The idea of technique

In the world of psychotherapy and counselling it is far from unusual to encounter the idea that there is something called 'technique' and that good therapy requires the mastering of this and its appropriate deployment. Alongside this often goes the idea that the therapist must be 'flexible' in how he or she works. In this chapter I want to put these ideas into question, not because I believe that therapists should be inflexible, but because the idea that there is something called technique (and therefore 'flexibility of technique') in the practice of psychotherapy and counselling is fundamentally misconceived.

The word technique has come to be associated in our minds with 'technical', that is with the mechanical or the scientific. Even though the dictionary defines technique primarily as pertaining to artistic execution or performance, this is still related to what the dictionary calls the 'formal or practical' details as distinct from 'general effect, expression, sentiment, etc.'. The *Shorter Oxford English Dictionary* cites the musicologist Grove to the effect that 'a player may be perfect in technique, and yet have neither soul nor intelligence'. Technique, in other words, relates to the mechanical, practical or formal aspect of the art as opposed to what one does with these. How one strikes the keys, plucks the strings, or applies the paint to the canvas are not the same as the art that may result. It is a pity perhaps that this is what the word has come to mean for technique, after all, derives from the Greek, *tekne* which means art or craft. Sadly, the word has come to have other meanings and it may be impossible to retrieve it. Far better perhaps to speak of the art of psychotherapy or counselling rather than technique.

So the notion that there might be something called a technique of psychotherapy, at least in the sense of a 'technical practice', is highly misleading. This is so not only because every patient is different, a unique individual with her or his unique personal history, but because every psychotherapist is also unique, with her or his own particular way of working and way of being with others. The notion implied by a great many counselling and psychotherapy texts that there is a technique or techniques for dealing with people who are seen to belong to a particular group (the elderly, the young, women, gays, lesbians, and so on) or as presenting apparently similar forms of emotional distress (depression, anorexia, cutting, and so on) is seriously misguided.

As a number of writers, including John Heaton, Peter Lomas and David Smail, have argued, psychotherapy is not and cannot be a matter of technique in the sense of the scientific application of protocols. For a start, there are just too many different theories of psychotherapy. They cannot all be right and indeed a great many are mutually exclusive and cannot be incorporated under some embracing umbrella of 'eclectic'. But there is no evidence to suggest that any one model of psychotherapy is any better at helping people than any of the others. What matters, what makes a difference to people, is the person of the therapist.

The idea of a psychotherapeutic technique or techniques therefore becomes deeply problematic. However, as Peter Lomas argues in *Doing Good? Psychotherapy Out of its Depth*, the attraction is that it is very much easier to formulate a technique than it is to 'articulate the nature of wise behaviour' (Lomas 1999: 19). What precisely, Lomas asks, is the nature of such 'technique'? The attempted practice of a technique, he argues, results in simplification. It implies that there are certain lines of action considered desirable and necessary and others which are to be avoided, which diverts one's attention from anything other than what one has been taught to look for. How else can practitioners from so many different schools find 'proof' for their positions from exactly the same material? In this respect, John Heaton gives the example of a married woman in analysis who began an affair and was told by her analyst that she was acting out transference fantasies; but a second analyst sees her behaviour in terms of a freeing of her sexuality. The profession of psychotherapy, Heaton remarks, seems to attract people for whom a single perspective is authoritative. They do not see that they are actors in a drama, much of whose script has already been written in the theories of the particular school to which they adhere (Heaton 1999: 74–6).

This does not mean that one cannot study psychotherapy or even draw generalisations from the observations made, but it does mean, as David Smail has argued, that such generalisations cannot be turned into prescriptions for the detailed conduct of the therapy itself. What one is reading when a psychotherapist is writing about her or his work is how *that person works*. What happens between therapist and patient or client is essentially personal and therefore unique to the parties involved: 'It does not make any sense to try to professionalise what is after all a kind of human relating. It would be as sensible to try to professionalise marriage' (Smail 1999: 135).

Freud's *Papers on Technique*

What then, it might be asked, of Freud's *Papers on Technique* (1911–1914)? Do these not lay persuasive claim to the idea that there is a technique in the practice of psychotherapy? Freud believed that the papers he wrote on technique – for example, 'Recommendations to

Physicians Practising Psychoanalysis', 'On Beginning the Treatment', 'The Dynamics of Transference' and 'Observations on Transference Love' – contained the essence of what every would-be psychoanalyst needed to know about the aims and methods of analysis. But as Mike Thompson has shown in *The Truth About Freud's Technique*, these papers, far from constituting some kind of 'technical manual' for the practice of psychotherapy, are in fact more in the nature of personal advice from Freud:

> Freud stated that the rules – in fact, recommendations – that he advocated for the practice of psychoanalysis were suited to his personality. Other analysts were urged to be flexible when attempting to apply his recommendations to their own. In other words, their technique should suit their personalities, just as Freud's suited his ... Analysts couldn't be told *how* to conduct analysis, they could only be offered 'fatherly advice' about what they could expect and the hazards they might wish to avoid. Freud's conception of technique was very subtle, and very personal ... he realised it had to be faithful to who the practitioner happens to be. Artists can be taught how to paint, but they can't be taught how to create, that is, how to be artists – neither can psychoanalysts. Artists who never learn – who never discover – how to paint for themselves will only paint mechanically, predictably, and poorly. The same is true of analysts. They're on their own when it comes to becoming psychoanalysts, in their fashion and in their person.
>
> (Thompson 1994: 138–9)

Classical psychoanalysis, Thompson remarks, at least as it is currently defined, is not what Freud himself practised. Many years after writing the 'technical papers' Freud wrote to Ferenczi on the problem of advising analysts what they should do when in fact they need to determine it for themselves:

> Recommendations on technique I wrote long ago were essentially of a negative nature. I considered the most important thing was to emphasise what one should *not* do, and to point out the temptations in directions contrary to analysis. Almost everything positive that one *should* do I have left to 'tact' ... The result was that the docile analysts did not perceive the elasticity of the rules I had laid down and submitted to them as if they were taboos.
>
> (Freud, quoted in Thompson 1994: 138–9)

The idea of rules in psychotherapy

Although few people might actually use the word, the idea that there are rules for the practice of psychotherapy is a widespread one, and not only among trainees and the less experienced. But what are these rules? And what person or what body could possibly lay down rules and with what authority? Take for instance the idea that the therapeutic hour should last 50 minutes. Is it a rule that it should? If it is, who laid it down? Whose authority lies behind it? The truth is that the 50-minute duration is a practice that many psychotherapists and counsellors follow, although many do not. I have known psychotherapists who give people 55 or even 60 minutes, others who use extended sessions of 90 minutes with some clients, either for practical reasons because they live some distance away and travel is difficult, or because they seem to need this kind of time. It is also the case that in other parts of Europe, France for instance, the standard length of the psychotherapy session is not 50 minutes, but 45.

Take too the idea that therapy should be paid for. Is this a rule? Here we can, if we wish, cite our favourite authority, Freud, for this. Freud believed that free treatment increased resistance in the patient because it took the treatment away from the real world. However, as is well known, Freud himself made exceptions and even supported the 'Wolf Man' when he fell on hard times (Thompson 1994: 164). There is, I think, nothing intrinsically wrong with charging people for therapy, which is not to say that I do not think there are serious problems arising from the fact that, whatever else therapy is, it is also a commercial transaction; nor to deny that there should be much greater treatment freely available within the NHS and in the voluntary sector than there is at present. But the idea that payment is somehow essential to the 'success' of therapy is spurious and self-serving.

Even the idea of regularity of sessions, while preferable, is not always possible. It can be simply impossible for people working flexible shift patterns to stipulate a time in normal working hours when they will always be free. The 'rule' that patients should lie down on a couch was, in part, advocated by Freud because he hated being stared at all day long.

As the Scottish psychoanalyst W.R.D. Fairbairn wrote, some features of psychoanalytic 'technique' exist not in the interests of the patient, but in the interests of the analyst (although presumably what is good for the therapist may also be good for the patient). There is nothing wrong with this. Therapists have needs too – to have breaks in the working day, to take holidays, to be paid reasonably for what we do and so on. The important thing is to acknowledge that this is so and not pretend otherwise (Fairbairn 1958: 378). The 50-minute hour is a reflection of the therapist's need for a break between sessions. There is nothing therapeutically magical about it. So too, there is nothing wrong with the fact that I need patients to pay me if I am to make a living, but this is my need, not the patient's. It is good for me, not for her. Much of the literature on this strikes one as self-pleading and self-interest disguised as concern for the patient.

What are often considered 'rules' are in truth conventions, that is commonly adopted ways of working. The only 'rules', in other words, that exist in the practice of psychotherapy are those that we make for ourselves. This does not mean that each psychotherapist has to start all over again, reinventing the wheel of therapeutic practice as it were; it would be foolish and arrogant to ignore the body of thought that has gone into these matters. But in the end one makes one's own 'rules of practice' for oneself: the duration of one's sessions, the fees one charges, what to do about cancellations and missed appointments, the length of breaks, and so on. In fact, it is probably better to avoid the word rule altogether. What we adopt, what we develop, simply constitutes our own way or ways of working.

Working in an institution

The therapist working in an institutional or organisational setting is not however a free agent but must abide by the rules or conventions of the organisation. Thus, for instance, it may be impossible to see clients more than once a week even if greater frequency is indicated by the nature of their difficulties or distress. Conversely, it may be impossible to agree to see people less often than weekly, even if this is all they may be able to manage, if this is the organisation's way. So too therapists working limited hours may not be able to offer changes of session times if someone is unable to make their usual time. It may also be impossible to extend the time of a session, for whatever reason, by more than a few minutes since this may interfere with the next person's session. In other words, therapists have to fit into and work within the structures of the organisation, as indeed do their clients.

It is common for therapists to be quite strict about clients arriving at and leaving their sessions on time and to regard lateness as a sign of some kind of 'pathology' or acting out. Some years ago, I was offering psychotherapy to clients of the Medical Foundation for the Care of

Victims of Torture. It was quite common for people to turn up very late for their appointments, 30 minutes, 40 minutes, even after their session had ended. So what was I to do? Allow them only the time left and try to explore the meaning of their lateness and explain the importance of coming on time? Send away those who had missed the whole session time? Or make up the time in some way knowing that this would inconvenience the next person, if indeed, he had arrived on time? Also, allowing someone extra time might mean keeping a room that had been allocated to someone else. Yet there were very good reasons why people might have arrived late. These were people who were used to being kept waiting, often for very long periods of time, at doctors' surgeries, at hospitals, at benefits offices, at immigration interviews. It was understandable, indeed to be expected, that they might not wish to add another source of being kept waiting. My point is that the strictures of the therapy frame did not necessarily work in the interests of these clients, but against them.

But an organisation is not just about these practical structures, many of which, if not most, may be unavoidable given the limited resources available. As I said at the head of this chapter, organisations also have cultures, ways of working, of their own, expressed in the idea not always explicitly articulated that 'this is the way we do things here'. This way of doing can include what is supposed to happen in the session itself. There is, in other words, a belief that there is a way of working that individual therapists are supposed to adopt, a way of doing therapy. This way of working usually derives from some strongly held theoretical position. In this context, therapy becomes a set of technical procedures to be applied in a mechanical fashion. The therapist who does not adhere to this dominant theoretical position is faced with the difficulty of trying to be true to himself as a therapist, to work as he wishes to work with his clients, to respond to them as he feels they are to be responded to, and yet face criticism from supervisors or peers for not doing as they would do. Thus, for instance, he might find himself criticised for answering a personal question directly, or for agreeing to waive a financial contribution, or for failing to interpret something in a particular way, or for not advising a third party, such as a GP, about something, and so on.

Contrary to such dogmatic approaches, I have come more and more to understand psychotherapy as an ethical endeavour in the sense of 'ethics' articulated by the French/Jewish philosopher Emmanuel Levinas, that is we are called upon to respond to the other who presents herself before us, seeking help. I have developed this line of thought at greater length elsewhere (Gordon 1999). Levinas proposed an understanding of our being in the world and, above all else, our way of being *with others* that is radically at odds with established thought. In particular, Levinas argued that ethics is responsibility for the Other and that this responsibility precedes knowledge. Such responsibility has, moreover, nothing whatsoever to do with reciprocity, that is I do not do something in order to get something in return. Furthermore, Levinas argued, it is this ethical responsibility which *constitutes me as a subject*, it is the meaning of my subjectivity. Ethics, or an ethical stance, is not something tacked on afterwards, as it were, to my being.

Ethics, in the very particular sense that Levinas gives it, is at the heart of psychotherapy, but ethics in this sense requires that we abandon a great many preconceptions and assumptions about otherness and about our relations with others; that we have to develop an attitude or position of radical openness towards the other in all her strangeness and that avoids reducing the other to what is already known to us.

We cannot know in advance what the content of our responsibility towards the other will be, what it will require of us, what demands it will place upon us. Nor can we know beforehand *how* we should respond, what we shall have to do. There are no rules or codes to guide us. To use a word much loved by Levinas, we are *hostage* to the other. Indeed, rules and codes may be a means of defending ourselves from the extent of the responsibility. The kind of ethical responsibility that Levinas is talking about shuns codification and cannot be taught by formal teaching.

An attitude of true openness to the other means that we approach the other, as far as possible, without preconceptions and, above all, without a pre-existing framework of ideas or supposed 'understanding' into which the other will be made to fit. It means that we abandon diagnostic categories (narcissistic, depressive, and so on) and theoretical models of the mind or the personality. In their place, we try to *meet* this other and in attempting to meet this other we respond to who they are or who we think and feel they might be, all the time keeping this open to question and revision. We try to get to know them and what distresses them, what makes them feel ill at ease, not at home in the world or in themselves.

There are many ways of getting to know someone in the therapeutic encounter, many ways of being with them. So, for example, one does not sit in silence with everyone, although this may well be appropriate with some people. One also reaches out to where they are. Many people frown on the asking of questions but how else do you find out things

– and more important how do you convey to someone that you are interested in them, what they are thinking, what they are feeling, what they are going through. Of course, asking questions can be oppressive and counter-productive. Tact and sensitivity are of the essence. But unless one is prepared to engage in trying to get to know someone, one might as well give up. As Peter Lomas puts it, therapists have to be prepared to engage in 'the tentative, risky, tactful, revealing, confronting and innumerable other attitudes that go along the path to intimacy' (1994: 198).

This getting to know someone may also involve an element of that horror of so many therapists, self-disclosure. By this I do not mean that the therapist takes over the therapy, but I do mean allowing oneself the freedom, for instance, to answer questions openly and honestly and to share one's own experience, if this feels appropriate *with the particular person*. I am not advocating a general 'rule' of disclosure. This does not preclude exploring what the asking of the question means, nor what it means to be given the information sought. Such disclosure may include the use of the feelings evoked in the therapist in the session – boredom, irritation, panic, sadness, nothing – in order to get at what the client may be feeling but is unable, for whatever reason, to put into words. Such states of feeling, as is now widely recognised, may well be important communications from the client. The psychoanalyst Paula Heimann stated the matter clearly in her seminal paper published 50 years ago: 'The analyst's emotional response to his patient within the analytic session represents one of the most important tools for his work. The analyst's counter-transference is an instrument of research into the patient's unconscious . . . If an analyst tries to work without consulting his feelings, his interpretations are poor . . . his counter-transference . . . is the most dynamic way in which his patient's voice reaches him' (Heimann 1950: 81–2).

Some examples

Let me try and give some sense of what I mean with a few examples based on my experience from 1993 to 1999 at Open Door, a psychotherapy service for young people in London. These examples are fictitious in the sense that they are constructions. The material on which they are based, however, is true. I have tried to describe at greater length the impact upon the therapist of working in this setting elsewhere (Gordon 2000).

David says little, volunteers even less. Trying to get anything from him is like getting blood out of a stone. I ask the questions that I usually put to people in first meetings: What made him seek help now? What does he want? What does he imagine therapy might be like? What difficulties does he have in his life? What interests him? All to no avail. I feel stonewalled and I begin to feel like an interrogator. I don't like the way I am being. Yet to leave him in silence would, I feel, be to abandon him. If indeed he lasted the session he would be unlikely to return. He has come for help – he needs to be given it. The problem, of course, is precisely how to offer this help, how to engage with him without putting him through an interrogation. My spirits lift a little when, somehow, we alight on the subject of music. He listens to it a lot. My interest in his interest seems to surprise him but he talks a little bit more freely. Within minutes he finds himself talking about something that has bothered him for years, something that happened a few years before, that he has never before told anyone about. I feel touched and pleased that he is, despite himself perhaps, trusting me and the therapy.

For months, Cameron was the first of my evening clients. I would frequently struggle through rush hour traffic to arrive on time to see him, only to be told that he had rung 5, 10, 15 or even 40 minutes earlier to cancel his session, that is once I was on my way to see him. He rarely just missed a session by not turning up. It was too easy to say that he was 'attacking the therapy', even though this may have been part of the truth. But the truth was also that he was keeping in touch, letting me know he had the therapy in mind. I recalled something Patrick Casement had written about a therapist whose patient was often late or missed sessions and how he had encouraged the therapist always to 'make a point of *starting every session on time with or without the patient*'. In this way she would be exposed most directly to different forms of absence (Casement 1990: 23). Following this advice I would sit in my room trying to monitor what I was feeling and to experience what Casement calls 'communication by impact', that is the way in which by his absence a client may be attempting to evoke in the therapist a resonance to his own difficult feelings (Casement 1985: 89). Sitting in the room in Cameron's absence, I too could speculate about what might be going on for him – anger, frustration, a sense of uselessness. The problem was, of course, that unless he did eventually come there was nothing I could do with my thoughts, except bear the feelings aroused in me.

Zoe was young and pretty and flirtatious. She would attend one or two sessions then miss one, usually without notice. I would then be in the position of wondering, and indeed sometimes worrying, about what had happened to her and having to decide after each missed session what to do. Should I write to her or even phone her? If I did either of these was I running the risk of being seen to be seductive or pressuring if I did contact her or, on the other hand, uncaring and abandoning if I did not.

For many sessions after her first one, Juliet found it almost imposs- ible to speak to me. My questions or musings about what she might be thinking or feeling seemed painful to her, intrusive. I learned that what she needed was for me to be there, in the room with her, attentive and alert until she felt moved to tell me, in her own time and in her own way, her terrible story.

Joseph wanted something altogether different. He wanted me to be involved with him, to meet him, as he would put it. He wanted honesty from me and would frequently ask my opinion about something he had said about himself. To hide behind a mask of therapeutic neutrality, he made clear, was no use to him. Very gradually, I began to allow myself to get more real with him, constantly fighting off super egoish voices telling me off. After a shaky start, the therapy took off and when Joseph eventually left he and I were in no doubt that it was precisely the 'realness' of our relationship, a realness that in no way precluded questioning and interpreting what was going on, that had made a difference.

In none of these instances was I adopting and utilising a technique, whether this be a technique of involvement with Joseph, a technique of distance with Juliet, or a technique of patience with Cameron. The very idea is absurd, just as the idea of a technique for any kind of relationship – spouse, lover, friend – is absurd. I was, rather, responding to different people in different ways, ways that seemed to me to be appropriate to the situation, to how they were at the time. I was being – or at least trying to be – open to the specific other with whom I found myself. This is rather different, I think, from being 'flexible', which suggests a norm or fixed point from which one may bend or vary but which privileges the norm or fixed point.

As I indicated above, one of the challenges facing the therapist working in an institutional setting is the challenge to be oneself, to paraphrase Bion, to dare to be the therapist that one is or might be. This can bring one into conflict with one's colleagues. At the very least it can be difficult to sit in one's room with clients and not find oneself wondering: 'Should I be saying this kind of thing? or 'How will this sound in the weekly clinical meeting? or 'How on earth will I present this to my supervisor?' Yet one owes it to oneself and one's clients to follow one's own intuition. Indeed, as a therapist as opposed to a technician, an applier of procedures, one cannot do otherwise.

There is, to be sure, nothing dramatic in what I was doing. Indeed, one might say that I was 'just being ordinary', but it is precisely through all the vagaries and complexities of being ordinary that change through therapy may come about.

References

Casement, P. (1985) *On Learning From the Patient*, London: Tavistock.
—— (1990) *Further Learning from the Patient: The Analytic Space and Process*, London: Routledge.
Fairbairn, W.R.D. (1958) 'On the nature and aims of psycho-analytical treatment', *International Journal of Psycho-Analysis* 39: 374–85.
Freud, S. (1911–1914) *Papers on Technique (Collected Works Vol. XII)*, London: Institute of Psychoanalysis and Hogarth Press.
Gordon, P. (1999) *Face to Face: Therapy as Ethics*, London: Constable.
—— (2000) 'Playing for time: a psychotherapist's experience of counselling young people', *Psychodynamic Counselling* 6: 339–57.
Heaton, J. (1999) 'The ordinary', in L. King (ed.) *Committed Uncertainty in Psychotherapy: Essays in Honour of Peter Lomas*, London: Whurr.
Heimann, P. (1950) 'On counter-transference', *International Journal of Psycho-Analysis* 31: 81–4.
Lomas, P. (1994) *Cultivating Intuition: An Introduction to Psychotherapy*, Harmondsworth: Penguin.
—— (1999) *Doing Good?: Psychotherapy Out of its Depth*, Oxford: Oxford University Press.
Smail, D. (1999) 'A century of psychotherapy', in L. King (ed.) *Committed Uncertainty in Psychotherapy: Essays in Honour of Peter Lomas*, London: Whurr.
Thompson, M.G. (1994) *The Truth About Freud's Technique: The Encounter with the Real*, New York: New York University Press.

Chapter 10

Counselling in a postmodern context

A possible role for community and voluntary counselling services

Quentin Stimpson

In this chapter I aim to consider community and voluntary counselling services from a postmodern perspective in order to see what possibilities this might open up for their future within a world increasingly concerned with evidence-based practice and cost-effective treatments. Throughout my argument will be informed by my own experiences of working with a range of voluntary and community-based counselling agencies over the past 14 years. In order to set out my thoughts it will be neccessary initially to establish what I mean by postmodernism (and indeed by implication modernism) before I address what I see as being a possible place for community and voluntary counselling services in a postmodern world.

Why postmodernism?

Our current world has been described as postmodern: 'it designates the state of our culture' (Lyotard 1984: xxiii), and the postmodern condition, although difficult to define, is characterised by the following elements (Gergen 1999: 195):

- a sense of life as being in a state of rapid transition (which is enhanced by the exponential growth and development of information technology);
- a sense of the 'self' as fragmented;
- the loss of 'traditional' values and certainties (which includes the death of 'grand narratives', i.e. the loss of faith in the promises to end all human suffering as offered by the great systems of thought and practice named science, religion and politics).

But to begin to understand what postmodernism might have to say to us today, it is necessary to consider what is meant by the term 'modernism'.

This is because postmodern themes are often seen as being in contrast to modernism's focus on such things as the primacy of the individual speaking subject and the development of science and technology as ways for humans to gain control and mastery over themselves and their environments (including the harnessing of the natural world) in order ultimately to eliminate human suffering in all its forms (Appignanesi and Garratt 1995: 11). Counselling and psychotherapy have been framed up as quintessentially modernist undertakings (e.g. Cushman 1992, 1995) to the extent that they aim at producing better, more competent, in control selves/people. In this way they become part of the modernist movement towards what Foucault termed 'disciplinary power' (1977): i.e. the production of selves/people willing to police and regulate their own behaviours by developing, in this case, internal mechanisms for controlling and moderating their wishes and desires. Following this line of thought to its logical conclusion leads to counselling and psychotherapy becoming packaged (Heaton 1993; Rose 1997) as a marketable set of theories and techniques designed to produce better, more desirable people. In this sense counselling and psychotherapy become the psychological counterparts to contemporary developments in human cloning and genetic engineering, although some would argue that such hard science practices and developments will ultimately make counselling and psychotherapy obsolete.

Counselling and psychotherapy have become caught up in this contemporary demand for scientifically validated, ever more sophisticated technologies (where power equals knowledge) in their attempts to subject themselves to the dictates of evidence-based practice. The need to answer the question 'what works most cost effectively for whom?' has become of paramount importance. This, of course, situates counselling and psychotherapy firmly within medicine, as quasi-medical treatments, and if successful this manoeuvre will provide a powerful validation of counselling and psychotherapy as they seek to gain statutory regulation and a legitimised professional status – or to put it more simply there's a lot at stake here.

It is at this point that I want to return to my question 'Why postmodernism?' and see what possibilities and challenges a postmodern perspective might open up in relation to the themes discussed above, while also considering the place of community and voluntary counselling services within these contemporary developments. As Bauman (1990: 272) notes, postmodernism is not essentially a separate entity apart from modernism but rather modern's extension and development, or as Elliott (1996: 3) puts it: 'Self-reflection on modernity is part and parcel of that "turning back against itself" that comes into existence with the advent of postmodernity.' Thus postmodernism opens up a critical, reflexive space where all truth claims can be seen for what they are, i.e. truth games, and the way in which knowledge is produced and promulgated can be deconstructed and critiqued in order to reveal the underlying assumptions, power and political dynamics that inform its construction. In other words, postmodernism problematises and politicises all knowledge and truth claims, which is usually achieved by approaching them, to borrow a phrase from Lyotard (1984) as 'language games'.

A postmodern perspective, building on the work of Foucault (e.g. Sarup 1993: 64), alerts us to how science becomes concerned with the process of deciding how something can be considered scientific rather than with discovering truth. Thus postmodernism encourages us critically to appraise what we are told is scientifically validated and to consider what it is that gets left out or marginalised. We are now in a position to question the current dedication to evidence-based practice: we have to begin to wonder about who decides what constitutes a successful outcome? On whose terms is this based – the client's or the therapist's, with their aspirations for professional status and need to demonstrate their technical, therapeutic prowess? After all, most case studies and research reports in the psychotherapy/counselling fields fail to give full weight to the experiences of the clients taking part in them. While the client may report a reduction in specific symptoms after a counselling or psychotherapy 'treatment', nobody usually takes the time to ask the client what that actually means to them (or, whether the reduction in symptoms is actually experienced by them as being helpful).

The problems of attempting to measure efficacy via the use of randomised control trials and then translate that into everyday clinical effectiveness continue to be well documented (e.g. Messer 2001; Sturdee 2001; Wessely 2001) and, as Heaton (2001: 239) notes, there are 'some matters which are extremely important in understanding human beings and their confusions but which are not easily quantifiable or formulated in propositions and so tend to be ignored by EBM' (EBM stands for evidence based medicine). Heaton demonstrates that there are many different types of evidence (including, for example, testimony and self-evidence); which is the best to base judgements upon in counselling and psychotherapy is not easy to decide. He then notes that in counselling and psychotherapy the relationship between the partcipants is of vital importance and along with this questions of love (so important to human beings) are often raised, but love is something about which evidence-based practice has nothing to say. Evidence-based practice is concerned with what can be generalised, not with specifics, and in this it is in danger of ignoring the particular client and their uniqueness.

The question arises as to whether it is possible to resist the onslaught of evidence-based practice and this is where I would suggest community and voluntary counselling services can make a vital contribution to the shaping of the counselling and psychotherapy. Community and voluntary counselling services work in diverse, localised contexts and attract clients who have either exhausted the resources of statutory provision or who actively wish not to be included within the framework of the statutory sector. Indeed as Robinson (this volume) notes, many community and voluntary counselling services developed as attempts at addressing the unmet needs of their local communities, where statutory provision was either lacking or unaccessible. It is this grass-roots, experience/need driven quality that makes community and voluntary counselling services uniquely placed to act as sites of resistance to the prevailing trends within counselling and psychotherapy highlighted above. If they can resist unquestioningly adopting the standards set by evidence-based practice, then it could be possible for them to devise more naturalistic, real-world research projects that could act as a counterbalance to the sterility of much randomised control trial based research. What I am suggesting is that community and voluntary counselling services can provide an important voice in the uncertain future of counselling and psychotherapy to the extent that they can claim to be attempts at meeting the client in their difference (not because they fit a diagnostic category or a referral procedure). The reporting of experiences gained from these real-world practice settings could contribute to the development of practice-relevant learning and the continued evolution of psychotherapeutic theory and practice.

Essentially, what I am suggesting is that the non-statutory nature of voluntary and community counselling services (their positioning in the margins, so to speak) is an important quality that could be used to create a reflective space where new learning can be generated, and otherwise taken-for-granted assumptions can be questioned (e.g. the desirability of evidence-based practice as a controlling force over the delivery of counselling services to clients). It is, of course, becoming extremely difficult for non-statutory services not to adopt the standards and practices of their 'professional' colleagues. As a counselling place-ments co-ordinator on an MSc counselling training course, I am only too aware of just how difficult it is becoming to find high quality placements for students beginning their counselling practice. Increasingly it seems that the standards which voluntary and community organisations are setting as basic entry requirements for their volunteer counsellors are at root quite high professional ones. All too often I find that students are faced with the realisation that they need at least several hundred hours of previous counselling practice in order even to be considered for a voluntary counselling placement, which raises the question of 'How do you get that experience if everyone insists that you already have it?' This would seem to be indicative of a more general trend, namely the erosion of the voluntary counselling sector within our society. While it is, of course, important that clients (and potential clients) receive high quality services it would surely be a pity if the diversity of practitioners working in the voluntary counselling sector became too limited (due to the constraints of ever more stringent entry requirements). It would, of course, be useful to pause a moment and consider the finding that research consistently presents us with: when it comes to the provision of competent, ethical and professional counselling/therapy services it is usually the most highly qualified, experienced and respected practitioners who are the serial client abusers, not trainee or novice practitioners (Jehu 1994). This would seem to be an argument for remaining sceptical about our competence as practitioners. Perhaps there is room for what in Zen is referred to as the importance of keeping a 'beginners's mind' (Suzuki 1949). This would suggest that it would make sense to devise well-managed schemes for trainee counsellors wishing to start their supervised counselling practice within voluntary counselling services (rather than automatically excluding them due to their lack of experience).

Voluntary counselling services are in a unique position that could allow them to explore what Levinas spoke of as 'the between of responsible relatedness' (Gans 1999). They aim at being open to the 'demand of the face of the other' (Gordon 1999) in that they seek to be accessible to clients as they present in their difference (a difference that is not only from the practitioner, but also from the practitioner's theories) and as such they are a place where 'otherness' can be encountered and acknowledged, rather than having violence done to it (Levinas 1969; Loewenthal 1996). It would be a great loss if voluntary (non-statutory) counselling services allowed themselves to be appropriated into mainstream, professional discourses rather than retaining a degree of sceptical independence where something different (sic alterity) can be given space and a voice.

References

Appignanesi, R. and Garratt, C. (1995) *Postmodernism for Beginners*, London: Icon Books.

Bauman, Z. (1990) *Modernity and Ambivalence*, Cambridge: Polity Press.

Cushman, P. (1992) 'Psychotherapy to 1992: a historically-situated interpretation', in D.K. Freedheim (ed.) *History of Psychotherapy: A Century of Change*, Washington, DC: American Psychological Association.

—— (1995) *Constructing the Self, Constructing America: A Cultural History of Psychotherapy*, New York: Addison-Wesley.

Elliott, A. (1996) *Subject to Ourselves*, Cambridge: Polity Press.

Foucault, M. (1977) *Discipline and Punish: The Birth of the Prison*, Harmondsworth: Penguin.

Gans, S. (1999) 'Levinas and the question of the group', in C. Oakley (ed.) *What is a Group?*, London: Rebus Press.

Gergen, K.J. (1999) *An Invitation to Social Construction*, London: Sage.

Gordon, P. (1999) *Face To Face: Psychotherapy As Ethics*, London: Constable.

Heaton, J. (1993) 'The sceptical tradition in psychotherapy', in L. Spurling (ed.) *From the Words of My Mouth*, London: Routledge.

—— (2001) 'Evidence and psychotherapy', *European Journal of Psychotherapy, Counselling and Health* 4, 2: 237–48.

Jehu, D. (1994) *Patients As Victims*, London: Wiley.

Levinas, E. (1969) *Totality and Infinity*, Penn: Duquense University.

Loewenthal, D. (1996) 'The postmodern counsellor: some implications for practice, theory, research and professionalism', *Counselling Psychology Quarterly* 9, 4: 373–81.

Lyotard, J.-F. (1984) *The Postmodern Condition: A Report on Knowledge*, trans. G. Bennington and B. Massumi, Manchester: Manchester University Press.

Messer, S.B. (2001) 'Empirically supported treatments: what's a nonbehaviourist to do?', in B.D. Slife, R.N. Williams and S.H. Barlow (eds) *Critical Issues in Psychotherapy*, London: Sage.

Rose, K. (1997) 'Counselling: product or process?', *Psychodynamic Counselling* 3, 4: 387–99.

Sarup, M. (1993) *An Introduction to Post-Structuralism and Postmodernism*, Harvester.

Sturdee, P. (2001) 'Evidence, influence or evaluation? Fact and value in clinical science', in C. Mace, S. Moorey and B. Roberts (eds) *Evidence in the Psychological Therapies*, London: Brunner-Routledge.

Suzuki, D.T. (1949) *The Zen Doctrine of No-Mind*, London: Rider.

Wessely, S. (2001) 'Randomised controlled trials: the gold standard?', in C. Mace, S. Moorey and B. Roberts (eds) *Evidence in the Psychological Therapies*, London: Brunner-Routledge.

Index